DATE DUE

NO 26 '97			
OC 2 '98			
DE 14 98			
DE 1 '99			
MAY 18 2004			
'JUN 09 2004			
OC 26 '10			

DEMCO 38-296

Soldaderas in the Mexican Military

R

SOLDADERAS
IN THE MEXICAN MILITARY

Myth and History

ELIZABETH SALAS

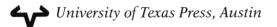 *University of Texas Press, Austin*

Copyright © 1990 by the University of Texas Press
All rights reserved
Printed in the United States of America

First Edition, 1990

Requests for permission to reproduce material from this
work should be sent to Permissions, University of Texas Press,
Box 7819, Austin, Texas 78713-7819.

∞ The paper used in this publication meets the minimum
requirements of American National Standard for Information
Sciences—Permanence of Paper for Printed Library Materials,
ANSI Z39.48-1984.

Library of Congress Cataloging-in-Publication Data

Salas, Elizabeth, date.
    Soldaderas in the Mexican military : myth and history / by
Elizabeth Salas. — 1st ed.
        p.   cm.
    Includes bibliographical references.
    ISBN 0-292-77630-6 (alk. paper). — ISBN 0-292-77638-1
(pbk. : alk. paper)
    1. Mexico—Armed Forces—Women—History. 2. Women
and the military—Mexico—History.   I. Title.
UB419.M6S25   1990
355'.0082—dc20   89-48597
                                                          CIP

For my mother, Elizabeth
For my sister, Anita
For the Salas family

Contents

Preface

When I was a graduate student at UCLA, someone asked me who the *soldaderas* were. I answered that they were both Mexican army women and Chicanas living in the United States. This fundamental observation has guided my research. I focused first on the antecedents of the *soldaderas* in Mesoamerican warrior societies and their mythification in religion as war goddesses. I then traced the *soldaderas'* involvement in most of Mexico's wars and armies well into the twentieth century.

Having covered the military history of women in armies, the next step involved analyzing the legacy of the *soldaderas*. This aspect of the study necessarily called for an interdisciplinary approach fusing history, literature, and popular culture. Because thousands upon thousands of Mexican women, over many centuries, participated in war, the meaning of their experiences varies extensively. For many Mexicans the *soldaderas* were fierce fighters for justice; for others, they were little more than miserable camp followers.

Chicanos and especially Chicanas show constant interest in learning about the *soldaderas* as part of the effort to maintain the cultural memory of their female ancestors from Mexico. At the same time, they too express diverse opinions about who the *soldaderas* were and what their legacy means for La Raza. This study, then, concerns itself with the different worlds of the *soldaderas* and the tremendous and continuing impact they have on people of Mexican descent.

Researching and writing about the *soldaderas* has been a fascinating adventure. As I tracked them through history, I received advice and help from many individuals. I would like to thank Robert Burr, Vicki L. Ruiz, Mario García, Kathryn Kish Sklar, Anne Walthall, Concepción Valadez, and Norris Hundley. Funding for parts of this study came from UCLA travel grants to Washington, D.C., a Tinker Foundation Summer Research Grant to Mexico City, and a University of California–Santa Barbara Chicana Dissertation Fellowship. The Chicano Studies Research Library at UCLA under the able leadership of Richard Chabrán, the National Archives and the Library of Congress in Washington, D.C., and the Departamento de Estudios Contemporáneos, Programa de Historia Oral (PHO), Archivo de la Palabra del Instituto Nacional de Antropología e Historia (INAH) in Mexico City all were filled with data that made a major difference in the presentation of this study. I thank University of Texas Press editors Kathryn Bork, Barbara Spielman, and, especially, Theresa May for their belief in this project.

My family has provided me with the secure environment and support system that I needed to complete this study. I remember well my father's and brothers' absorbing interest in all things of a military nature. It was my sister, Anita, who first urged me to write a book about the *soldaderas*. I recall with fondness my mother's stories about the strong women of my family: the grandmothers, Marcelina Salas Ortiz de Lewis, Emilia Candelaria de Lewis, and Merced Rangel de Salas, and their lives in New Mexico and Mexico. Finally, I thank my mother, Elizabeth, my mentor, for being the kind and loving person that she is to everyone she encounters.

Introduction

Armies, wars, and revolutions in Mexico have had a great impact on the lives of innumerable women since pre-Conquest times. Women warriors, camp followers, *coronelas*, *soldaderas*, and Adelitas are just some of the names given to these women.[1] Many of the tasks women performed in armies and during warfare correspond to those performed by men in the ranks and the quartermaster corps.

The fact that these women have no common label is a reflection of military thinking, which seeks to use women when necessary but yet keeps them marginal in what is essentially a male preserve. For this reason, the heroic camp follower or fighter of one war might be condemned as a prostitute or unnatural woman in another era.

In Mexican history, it is not considered appropriate to link legendary and historical figures, such as Coyolxauqhui, Malinche, Leona Vicario, the *coronelas*, and the *soldaderas* of the 1910 Revolution, when analyzing women's participation in armies and warfare. These women are usually classified separately, primarily to take into account time period and class.

Yet that is what this study intends to do—to link all Mexican women, regardless of era, class, or nom de guerre under a fundamental historical truth, that soldiering has over many centuries been a traditional and commonplace life experience for thousands of Mexican women. Constant warfare in Mexico from pre-Conquest times to the 1930s assured women many opportunities to show, willingly or unwillingly, their considerable skills in soldiering.

The seminal study about the *soldaderas* was written by Angeles Mendieta Alatorre (1961). Her work is an overview that cites mythical, historical, and literary female soldiers and patriots from ancient Mesoamerican history to the 1910 Revolution. Other notable works, by Gustavo Casasola (1960–1970), Anna Macías (1982), Shirlene Soto (1977), and Frederick C. Turner (1967), are limited to a discussion of *soldaderas* during and after the Revolution.

This study follows in the footsteps of Mendieta Alatorre and seeks to elaborate on the interchange between Mexican women caught up in constant wars and revolutions. An understanding of woman's roles in ritual and ancient warfare, as mother/war goddess, as intermediary and sexual companion to warriors, is important because *soldaderas* in many ways carried on these tribal defender duties for their people.

Both domestic and foreign troops after the Spanish Conquest in 1519 used women as servants. Soldiers used their pay (*soldada*) to employ women as paid servants (*soldaderas*). As *soldaderas* women gained some of their earliest work experience in wage labor. In general, *soldaderas* are incorrectly perceived as either wives or unpaid female relatives of the soldiers. Yet the semiofficial services they rendered to the soldiers took the form of transactions.

The soldiers would receive their pay and give it to the *soldaderas*, who as servants would purchase food and personal supplies. Working for soldiers became a way for poor, lower-class women to eke out a meager living for themselves and their children. Not bound by traditional marriage practices, they could travel the country with the armies, leave the soldiers they were serving at will, and at times earn extra money by additional work as laundresses, food sellers, and prostitutes.

By the time of the Revolution, nothing characterized the civil war more than the sight of thousands of *soldaderas* putting forth a dazzling display of their considerable talents as soldiers and camp followers. While the Revolution can be rightly considered the greatest of times for the *soldaderas*, by the 1930s they had been barred from the ranks, barracks, and field maneuvers; by the 1940s they had been redesignated as soldiers' wives by the government.

Besides an overview of the *soldaderas* during the Revolution, I place a separate focus on a Mexican army interned in U.S. forts during 1914. The Mexican army jailed at Fort Bliss and later at Fort Wingate from January to September consisted of 3,559 officers and soldiers, 1,256 *soldaderas,* and 554 children. This army of men and women came under critical scrutiny from U.S. Army officials and civilian observers.

It is crucial to the study of the *soldaderas* to include oral history, which can clarify what kind of impact soldiering had on women. Thus the experiences of nine women who participated in the Revolution are presented in this study.

Also important is the considerable impact that these women have had on Mexican music, literature, art, and film throughout the centuries. A common theme in these expressions of popular culture concerns the struggle to tame the *soldaderas* with romantic love or by fostering their reputations as loose women.

The imagery of the *soldaderas* has also had a profound impact on Mexicans who emigrated to the United States,[2] on the Chicano movement of the 1960s, and on American popular culture. The *soldaderas* appear as important characters in Mexican immigration sagas and Chicano literature. The Chicano movement used its own version of the *soldadera* as both a recruitment technique and a symbol to reinforce traditional Mexican womanhood. Euro-American filmmakers and popular novelists made the *soldaderas* characters in their works about Mexico. A debate developed and still continues among Chicanas about the value of the *soldadera* as an identity symbol.

Over the centuries, changes in the imagery of the *soldaderas* are tied directly to the evolution of the Mexican military from its Mexica (Aztec) and Spanish antecedents to the present-day army and to cultural reflections about the roles of Mexican women in conflicts.

Mesoamerican Origins 1

In myth Snake Woman was the war god's mother. She was there to trigger those wars over which her son, as the god of war, presided. He was the doer and the victory bringer, she the inciter.

—Burr Cartwright Brundage

In many Mesoamerican societies, women figured prominently as both war goddesses and legendary warriors. The connection between these myths and real women who engaged in warfare is often obscured by scholars. As Brundage shows, the study of war goddesses focuses on their symbolic roles as bloodthirsty demons and provocateurs of male warriors. Miguel León-Portilla, embellishing the same theme, surmises that the Mexicas believed that Ometeotl, the cosmic being, was both "father and mother" and in "his maternal role he was Coatlícue [the Great Mother] and Cihuacóatl [Snake Woman]."[1]

While war gods like Mixcóatl and Huitzilopochtli are thought to have been real male warrior leaders later deified into myth, the same conclusions are not drawn about the war goddesses, Cihuacóatl and Coyolxauhqui. Rather, war goddesses and female warrior leaders are viewed as mythical fantasies created by men and not at all reflective of women's varied roles over several centuries as tribal leaders, defenders, and warriors.

Motherhood was unquestionably the most important role for women in Mesoamerica. In mythical accounts, it was deified into a series of Earth Mothers who had tremendous powers for good and evil. Often in myth the Earth Mother's most common manifestation was as a war goddess. The fusion of the Earth Mother/war goddess in myth equates to a fundamental aspect of tribal life. Mesoamerican women lived in tribes that gradually migrated into the Valley of Mexico. Along the trek, both men and women helped lead and defend their tribe from enemies. This tribal tradition is reflected in religious myths about the Earth Mother who at certain times becomes a war goddess or tribal defender. This mother/war goddess combination appears in legends about Toci (Our Grandmother) and her warrior manifestation, Yaocihuatl (Enemy Woman), and was reinforced in later generations in various combinations such as Itzpapalótl/Itzpapalótl (Obsidian Knife Butterfly [both manifestations are warlike]), Serpent Skirt/Chimalman (Shield Hand), Coatlícue (Lady of the Snaky Skirt)/Coyolxauhqui (She Is Decorated with Tinkling Bells, Golden Bells), Coatlícue/Cihuacóatl (Snake Woman), and in later times Our Lady of Guadalupe/María Insurgente (Insurgent Mary).[2]

The Earth Mother/war goddess fusion emerged from the political, economic, and social structure of many early Mesoamerican tribes wherein some powers related to inheritance, property, and tribal defense passed from mother to daughter. Don Fernando de Alva Ixtlilxochitl, a Mexica himself, remarks that at Tula (an ancient center of civilization), "women had held supreme power."[3] Eric Wolf notes the possibility that in some early cultures "descent through females provided the main organizing principle of social life."[4] Women, as the strategic sex in reproduction and production and gathering of food, could hold power because "property in houses, goods and crops" often passed through female lines.[5] Women's powers extended, often out of necessity, to include that of warrior or tribal defender.

Artifacts of Toci (the most ancient Earth Mother deity from the Valley of Mexico), known as "Our Grandmother" by later tribes, depict her armed with a shield in one hand and a broom in the other, perhaps symbolizing the dominance of woman as domestic chief (mother) and war chief (daughter). The most common form for Toci was as a goddess of war named Yaocihuatl. The name Yaocihuatl, which means Enemy Woman, probably was used by later generations of male warrior nations to discredit female warriors. It is quite possible that Yaocihuatl was in real life or in myth the "daughter Amazon" or war chief of the tribe.[6]

Itzpapalótl and her warlike manifestation, of the same name, come from the ancient Chichimeca tribes that migrated from the far north to the Valley of Mexico. Described as having a fleshless face and talons instead of hands and feet, she was closely identified with war and hunting. She is referred to as an "authentic Chichimeca deity" in that "she was never tamed."[7] This description suggests that Chichimeca women were acknowledged fighters who defied defeat.

In many instances it was necessary for women to fight in defense of their families, kinship groups, and property. Tribes that migrated into the Valley of Mexico after A.D. 800 often faced constant intertribal warfare. Both men and women had to aid in the common defense of the tribe, with women fighting in three ways: as individuals, together with men, or in separate women's groups led by women. Over time, defense of tribes evolved into protection of towns and the nation.

There is some archeological evidence of female tribal defenders. Totonac figurines found in the vicinity of Veracruz (ca. A.D. 600–800) depict women as "veritable Amazons, bare waisted, serious faced, carrying shields and wearing huge headdresses."[8] More substantive evidence of female tribal defenders comes from legends of the Toltecs, the cultural progenitors of the Mexicas. Women fought side by side with men for Topiltzin until the tribe was destroyed in A.D. 1008.[9]

The Selden Codex (ca. A.D. 1035) tells the legend of the Warrior Princess. The story line accompanying the pictographs states:

> According to legend, men were born from trees. But Princess Six Monkey has parents of flesh and blood. Upon defending his kingdom, her father, Ten Eagle–Stone Tiger, takes the nobleman Three Lizard prisoner, but loses his three sons. Upon advice from the priest Six Buzzard the princess decides to defend her right to the throne . . . she becomes the wife of Prince Eleven Wind. . . . The priest Two Flower takes the princess to her husband's town. On the way, enemies of the princess insult her . . . the priestess Nine Grass advises her to punish the rebels. The ones who insulted her are taken prisoner by Six Monkey. Sweet revenge. Sacrifice of the chieftain. Six Monkey and Eleven Wind live happily ever after.[10]

The story shows that a priestess told Six Monkey that she should use force to defend her honor and the right to her father's kingdom. A woman who defended her people by creating and leading a women's battalion is Toltec Queen Xochitl (ca. A.D. 1116). The wife of Tecpancaltzin, Xochitl called women for military service and led them into a battle that cost her life.[11]

While some ancient myths depict female warriors holding their own with male warriors, other myths stress the dominance of the male warrior. Such is the case with the changing story about the origin of the Mexicas. Early in their wanderings, women played a significant role. The Mexicas in fact named themselves after Mecitli (Maguey Grandmother), a symbol of immense fecundity. In an early version of the myth of origins it is said that the Mexicas began "their wandering with two deities—Mecitli and a male form of Mixcóatl."[12]

As the Mexicas progressed farther into the Valley of Mexico, the myth of their origins was updated. The Earth Mother became Serpent Skirt and her warlike manifestation, or daughter, bore the name of Chimalman. This story focused on the confrontation between Chimalman and a more mature Mixcóatl (ca. A.D. 900). Mixcóatl set out to conquer new lands (in the state of Morelos) and found himself facing the region's warrior goddess Chimalman. Even though he was a powerful warrior, Mixcóatl's four arrows (the symbol for taking possession of new lands) did not kill Chimalman, as she was able to deflect them from her body. She then "shot her arrows and darts" at him without success. Chimalman returned to her caves but had to surrender after "Mixcóatl had raped her nymphs (servants)."[13]

Some time after entering the Valley of Mexico, perhaps in A.D. 1143, the Mexicas dethroned a prominent female warrior leader named Coyolxauhqui. While little is known about the real Coyolxauhqui, in myth she is said to be the Amazon daughter of the Earth Mother Coatlícue, her avatar and a titan. The male warrior who fought Coyolxauhqui and her many brothers for power and control of the Mexicas was the youngest brother, Huitzilopochtli. Allied with him was the Earth Mother Coatlícue.

The conflict suggests a shift away from the mother/daughter mythical relationship to a mother/son relationship. The suggested cause of the conflict may have been a rift between Coatlícue, the matriarch, and Coyolxauhqui, her Amazon daughter. Coyolxauhqui may have rebelled against Coatlícue to establish a more systematic and rational way to govern the tribes. According to Adela Formoso de Obregón Santacilia, Coyolxauhqui "ordered the end to warfare and warrior groups" and called for the "establishment of cities not based on warfare."[14]

Another view of the mythical conflict involves sibling rivalry among the children of Coatlícue. Huitzilopochtli, the youngest brother, was the personification of a "sexual revolution" in which men came into dominance as warriors and war chiefs. In order to redefine "civilization" along male lines, Huitzilopochtli seized on the conflict between Coatlícue and Coyolxauhqui to assert himself as a powerful war chief with a new destiny for the Mexicas.[15]

The Crónica Mexicayotl, written by Fernando Alvarado Tezozomoc (a Mexica) in 1609, cites the reasons for the revolution: "And the reason Huitzilopochtli went off and abandoned his sister, named Malinalxoch [another name for Coyolxauhqui] along the way, . . . was because she was very evil. She was an eater of people's hearts, an eater of people's limbs—It was her work—a bewitcher of people."[16] Coyolxauhqui allegedly used magic to hurt the opposition. The redefined "destiny" of the Mexicas under the new war chief Huitzilopochtli, according to Tezozomoc, was to continue warfare: "When I came forth, when I was sent here, I was given arrows and a shield, for battle is my work. And with my belly, with my head [references are to sacrifice of humans], I shall confront the cities everywhere. . . . Here I shall bring together the diverse peoples, and not in vain, for I shall conquer them."[17]

While the battle to depose Coyolxauhqui was successful, Huitzilopochtli was not yet powerful enough to challenge the Earth Mother Coatlícue for complete control. Instead, homage to Coatlícue and her war manifestation, Cihuacóatl, the "inciter" of war, was still necessary.

As the Mexicas gained greater control of the Valley of Mexico a more complex, male-dominated religious, military, and bureaucratic state developed. But the change from a past where women could be warriors and war chief to male dominance in these areas was an uneven process. The Earth Mother/war goddess combination that the Mexicas reinterpreted to suit their growing patriarchy shows that change took time and involved the destruction of their reputation. The next step in the severance of the people from the Earth Mother/war goddess cult was to make the latter into monsters. So it was that the Mexicas created the Earth Mother Coatlícue (her statue is a monstrosity) and her warlike manifestation, Cihuacóatl (blood drips from her shark-toothed mouth). In the "Song of Cihuacóatl," found in the Florentine Codex (1570), male warriors prayed to Cihuacóatl for a good war:

> Our Mother
> War Woman
> Deer of Colhuacán
> In plumage arrayed

> The sun proclaims the war
> Let men be dragged away
> It will forever end
> Deer of Colhuacán
> In plumage arrayed[18]

Even though the war chief, Huitzilopochtli, called for battle, he still had to ask Coatlícue and Cihuacóatl to rouse warriors.

The Mexicas, according to Brundage, merged the previous war goddesses Yaocihuatl and Coyolxauhqui with Cihuacóatl. In the Florentine Codex, she is even further discredited as the "savage Snake-woman, ill-omened and dreadful, who brought men misery."[19] Cihuacóatl, it was said, "giveth men the hoe and the tumpline. Thus she forceth men to work. And when she appeared before men, she was covered with chalk, like a court lady with obsidian earplugs. She was in white, having garbed herself in white, in pure white. Her tightly wound hairdress rose like two horns above her head. By night she walked weeping and wailing, a dread phantom foreboding war."[20] This description of Cihuacóatl would later be the basis of the very popular Mexican legend of La Llorona (the weeping woman). In this myth, a crying woman roams the night searching for her lost children or seeking revenge against men who have dethroned, sexually abused, or abandoned her.

The downfall of the warrior woman goddess had its human correlation in the barring of women from the office of war chief/co-ruler, also named Cihuacóatl. The supposition that women once held the office of war chief is not a popular one; scholarship on this possibility is decidedly negative. The Mexicas complicated the question by providing no explanation of the origins of the name Cihuacóatl. Even though in translation it means "Snake Woman," the explanation given by León-Portilla is questionable. He thinks that the name is simply Mexica acknowledgement of the "feminine" aspect of all men and not linguistic evidence that women were war chiefs. This analysis does not explain why, after a military victory, Cihuacóatl had to enter the occupied city dressed in women's clothing known as the "eagle garments." This practice was noted in the taking of the city of Quetzaltepec during the reign of Moctecuzoma Xocoyotzin (1502–1521).[21] The enactment of this ritual reflects homage to the ancient past, when female warriors probably held the position of war chief.

Not only did the Mexicas eliminate the warrior goddess and forbid women to be war chiefs but they also encouraged women not to bear arms in combat. *Mociuaquetzque* (valiant women) accompanied warriors into battle. They were described by sixteenth-century historian Fray Juan de Torquemada as intermediaries interspersed among the warriors in battle.[22] Their function on the battlefield is highly speculative. Possibly they acted as unarmed "neutrals" who coached and cheered on their warrior mates. If the *mociuaquetzque* kept to the "no-fighting" requirements of the ritual and were killed in battle, they were honored as brave women and guaranteed a place in the heaven reserved for warriors.[23]

The *mociuaquetzque* were not the only women who were called warriors and who had the opportunity to go to warrior's heaven. Women who gave birth were called warriors because the child coming out of the womb was covered with the mother's blood.[24] A Mexica woman who, along with her baby, died in childbirth was honored as a warrior who took a life. She and others like her were called *cihuapipiltin* (princesses) and in warrior's heaven they served as ritual guides to Huitzilopochtli as he (the sun) rose in the sky. In keeping with the Mexica strategy of honoring warlike activities of women while at the same time making them into monsters, the princesses were believed to appear at crossroads and paralyze people.[25]

The widowed husband, his friends, all the midwives, and old women armed with shields and swords had to guard her human remains from abduction by young male warriors. If the male warriors did steal the body of a dead woman, they cut off the middle finger of the left hand and took her hair. It was thought that these relics had magical power and, if placed on their shields, would make the warriors brave and valiant, give them strength, and "blind the eyes of their enemies."[26] Yet another explanation could be that warriors wanted the left middle finger of the woman because in earlier times, left-handed women had excelled as archers.

The religious ceremony of the ancient goddess Toci also shows that the change from a female warrior past to an exclusively male warrior society was still evolving. The feast of Toci took place on September 16, or the eleventh month, called Ochpaniztli (sweeping). It celebrated both woman's domestic concerns and her warlike abilities. The first part of the feast was dedicated to the goddesses of the earth and vegetation. Everyone got together to sweep and clean the areas surrounding the temples. The next part of the feast featured a mock battle between women. One woman chosen to impersonate Toci was then sacrificed. She was beheaded and then skinned. The ceremony concluded with a parade of new warrior recruits and warriors who received badges or weapons from the emperor.[27]

When the Mexicas expanded their empire, they still faced hostile tribes who used women in the thickest of fighting to try to shock the Mexicas and thereby delay the total defeat of their forces. One such incident took place in the reign of Mexica ruler Axayacatl (1469–1481). The war was against King Moquihuix of Tlatelolco. To gain time for the warriors to regroup, Moquihuix ordered a large group of women to take their clothes off and form a squadron. "They were made to attack the Mexica who were fighting furiously. The women, naked with their private parts revealed and their breasts uncovered, came upon them slapping their bellies, showing their breasts and squirting milk at the Mexicas."[28] But the tactic only dismayed the Mexicas, and Axayacatl told his warriors not to harm the women but to take them captive.

As Mexica society became more warlike, woman's role in warfare centered on promoting or objecting to the war effort and providing both personal and sexual services to warriors. If a young boy tried to court a Mexica girl, the old women who accompanied maidens would chide him as a boy with long hair and an "evil-stinking forelock" rather than the hairstyle of a warrior. The old women would call him a coward, an undisciplined recruit, and a woman who never got away from the hearth. Such insults served to "torment young men into war" and prod them into battle.[29]

When a warrior husband went off to war, the wife performed many ceremonies based on superstition "as a sign of sadness and mourning."[30] At different times of day (midnight, dawn, midday, sunset) the woman would build a fire, then go out into the street and sweep. She would then take a bath without washing her face. She would prepare food to be placed before idols on the home altar and pray. These mourning rites might be interpreted as a form of protest against war. If a husband did not come back from a battle, the widow was in mourning for eighty days. At the funeral, women were hired to wail for those who died in war. The wailers had to be of noble lineage and were joined in the lamentations by the widows, concubines, and other old women.[31]

The growth of the Mexica military empire necessitated larger numbers of men committed to warfare. This evolution of the Mexica army brought about an increase and acceptance of women as neutrals in battle and as *auianimes* (pleasure girls) specifically trained to provide sexual services for the warriors. Under the rule of Ahuitzotl, the *auianimes* were considered "public women who painted their faces in brilliant reds and yellows and chewed gum."[32] Fate decreed which Mexica girls would become *auianimes*. They were born during the rule of certain deities, most notably the goddess of sex, Tlazolteotl. As her slaves, they learned to dance, sing, and perform other acts of seduction. They wore different colors of paint on their faces and styled their hair in a way "that formed two little horns crossed on the forehead."[33]

The *auianimes* came not only from ill-fated Mexica women but from female war captives as well. The Mexicas considered the *auianimes* necessary to satisfy young men's sexual needs and to prevent marriage before the age of twenty. Early marriage was thought to "weaken the warrior."[34] Married warriors, known as *tequihuaque* (they who have important work to do), could keep mistresses and spend time with the *auianimes* "as a reward for risking their lives for the people."[35] The married warrior would give the *auianime* "color for her lips and cheeks, feathers for her head and jewels for her neck."[36] Mexica society looked down on "bad maidens and mature women," calling them "wicked, dishonored and gaudy."[37] Yet, possibly because of increased levels of warfare, they appear to have been tolerated, as quite a few Mexica women lived as *auianimes*. When the warriors came into a courtyard, the place "became filled to bursting with harlots, for there were many of these, and extremely shameless."[38]

Even though the *auianimes* may have been looked on with disdain, they were honored by being selected to be the dance partners of great warriors in the High Feast of the Dignitaries held in the eighth month, Uey Tecuihuitl. Officers and brave warriors skilled in warfare participated in this dance. The warriors "danced by pairs," and were joined by one of the *auianimes* "with her hair loose on her shoulders, dressed in a fringed, embroidered skirt."[39] On this occasion, the *auianimes* wore "no paint of any kind on their faces," thus suggesting how important and solemn the dance was for the dancers.[40] The *auianimes* were officially recognized and valued as members of society. However, once an *auianime* became ill with venereal disease or feeble from age, she was invited to a feast, asked to dance, and then strangled from behind.

On the eve of the Spanish Conquest, war goddesses were honored and celebrated in ceremonies where women symbolically displayed warlike abilities. But the growth of the Mexica empire saw the continuing decrease in the number of women fighting in battles, as exemplified by the *mociuaquetzque*. Other women accompanied the warriors to cook and carry supplies.[41] Increasingly, Mexica women served the military state by bearing sons to become fighters and daughters to become wives, mothers, or sexual companions to warriors.

Servants, Traitors, 2
and Heroines

*The women who followed the army merited all consideration, as they
did all they could to help the soldier. Some carried knapsacks, and
they would leave the road for a mile or two in the hot sun seeking
water; they prepared their food and even attempted to build huts
that would protect them from the elements.*

—*José Enrique de la Peña*

The Spanish, American, and French wars of conquest against Mexico from the sixteenth to the nineteenth centuries were brutal wars that necessitated and expanded the use of women in warfare. Both foreign and domestic armies used women as servants. Revolutionaries fighting foreign troops welcomed auxiliary and even armed support from women. At the same time, some officers wanted to restrict women's participation in their armies, because many women acted like regular soldiers rather than as obedient servants. Women who soldiered for foreign armies were often called traitors, while women who sided with domestic armies drew praise as heroines.

Women marched with soldiers for a variety of reasons, but primarily as wives. Just about any woman—for reasons of idealism, adventure, or simply survival—could work for one or more soldiers during her lifetime. Some women used the army to gain status or even marriage. Others were abducted or forced to work as army cooks and laundresses. Women's primary role in the army as domestic servants harks back to Mexica military practices. In the Mexica armies female camp followers followed the warriors to cook food and carry supplies. Many times the quartermaster corps, which included many women, was as large a force as the warriors.

The word *soldadera* came to Mexico courtesy of the Spanish Conquest. Spaniards from Aragón used *soldadera* for servants, either male or female, who took the soldier's pay, the *sold* or *soldada*, and bought him food and other supplies. It seems probable that *soldaderas* came from the lower classes.

The conflict between army officers and *soldaderas* centers on the issue of the exact nature of women's services to the army. This conflict became more apparent during the occupation of Mexico by foreign troops in 1519. From that time onward many women protested tactical maneuvers that expelled them from the army or the regular ranks and denied them battlefield promotions and pensions.

Spanish armies had their share of camp followers. About 1487 King Ferdinand banished from the army "the women and the camp followers who preyed upon the troops."[1] Queen Isabella herself reigned as a warrior monarch. In the Reconquest she often appeared on the battlefields "superbly mounted and dressed in complete armor."[2] Isabella supervised all military preparations and personally inspected every section of the Christian camp. Her special interest was the improvement of the artillery. She can also be credited with introducing the Queen's Hospitals, which consisted of four large hospital tents staffed with doctors, chemists, and surgeons.[3] Such involvement by a female ruler shows that warfare and soldiering were not solely the province of male rulers and strategists. While lower-class women often appeared in the camp follower ranks of Spanish armies, the example of Queen Isabella indicates that even an occasional upper-class woman could be a key architect of a military establishment.

Queen Isabella might well have served as an inspiration and role model for the twelve Castilian women who accompanied their husbands and fathers in the 1519 Conquest of Mexico: Beatriz Hernández, María de Vera, Elvira Hernández and her daughter Beatriz, Isabel Rodrigo, Catarina Márquez, Beatriz and Francisca Ordaz, María de Estrada, Beatriz Bermúdez de Velasco, Beatriz Palacios, and Juana Martín. Eight of the women were white, four were black. The four black camp followers reflects Spain's growing multiracial populace, resulting from the number of African slave and free persons residing in the country.

While these women were to perform domestic duties in the camps, the nature of warfare against indigenous tribes often placed them in the thick of battle. Subsequently, woman's role often expanded to include more soldierly duties. These twelve women nursed, stood guard, and in some instances fought alongside the Spanish soldiers. At least five were killed in battle.

In the initial days of the Conquest, Cortés wanted to prevent the Castilian wives from going on the march to the Mexica capital, Tenochtitlán (he wanted to leave them with his Indian allies in

Tlaxcala). But the women and even the men objected vehemently. The women declared that "Castilian wives, rather than abandon their husbands in danger, would die with them."[4] Bowing to this pressure, Cortés never issued the order.

By expressing fierce loyalty to their soldier-mates, the Castilian wives assured themselves tremendous adventures and, in some cases, access to prestige, land, and slaves. Beatriz Palacios, Beatriz Bermúdez, Isabel Rodrigo, María de Estrada, and Beatriz Hernández received attention because of their bravery and skill in warfare. Beatriz Palacios, known as "La Parda," was married to Pedro Escobar. Her nickname (*parda* means part black) refers to the probability that she was the daughter of an African mother and Spanish father. She "stood sentinel, tended the horses and the wounded, cooked, and did other things just like any other soldier."[5]

During the last battle for control of Tenochtitlán, Beatriz Bermúdez, wife of Francisco de Olmos, put on armor, a helmet and with sword and target, "ran out upon the causeway crying, for shame, for shame Spaniards, turn upon those base people, or if you will not, I will kill every man that attempts to pass this way."[6] Isabel Rodrigo, skilled in medicine, took care of the wounded soldiers. Blessed with a gift for healing, she would place her hands on the wounds of fallen soldiers and, with a blessing, the stricken soldiers would recover. For her services, the Spanish crown honored her with the title "Doctor" and she received permission to practice medicine in New Spain.[7]

María de Estrada's boldness and daring gained her two towns in Morelos. As the wife of Pedro Sánchez Farfán, she rode with the soldiers into battle and lanced many Mexica warriors. During a subsequent campaign in Morelos from 1522 to 1524, Cortés told his men that the soldier who led a charge against hostile Indians would be rewarded with an *encomienda* (land grant). Estrada "mounted a horse, took a lance and a leather shield and asked the Spanish captain for permission to attack the Indians and demonstrate her personal valor." Cortés granted her request and, "spurring on the horse, she attacked the enemy, yelling, 'Saint James, attack them!'"[8] It was a successful charge, as many Indians fled or fell into a ravine. True to his word, Cortés gave her the towns of Telala and Hueyapán.

Beatriz Hernández, wife of Captain Olea, accompanied her husband in the Conquest as well as in the campaign to settle Guadalajara. During the Mixtón War (1540–1541), Indians attacked the fledgling Guadalajara settlement continuously. On one occasion,

Hernández killed an Indian who successfully entered the fortified Spanish line of defense. The Indians tried to starve out the Spaniards and their Indian allies and also threatened to kill all the men and force the women into concubinage. Hernández had to be restrained by the men from leaping out of the protected area and slashing off the tongues of the Indians. After the siege had been lifted, it was Hernández who resolutely insisted that the town of Guadalajara be moved to a more defensible site, south of the Río Grande.[9]

Such actions reveal that Spanish and African women, though few in number, participated in the military conquest and settlement of Latin America. Their fierceness and resourcefulness show that lower-class women, unlike more socially restricted upper-class women, were used to surviving under harsh conditions. These women did not shrink from meeting new challenges and making their mark in the conquest of Mexico.

~ The most well known woman who soldiered during the Conquest was an Indian named Malinalli Tenepal. She gained her freedom, fame, and land for her aid to the Spaniards. Her status as a great *conquistadora* declined at exactly the same time that the Mexicans threw out the Spaniards in 1821. From that time onward, her reputation dwindled to that of a traitor. Her experiences are enlightening because, in spite of the terrible accusations made about her, no one has yet called her a *soldadera* or the prototype of the *coronela* of later generations. She has been cast as an ahistorical figure in Mexican history and myth.

Of noble heritage, Malinalli was born perhaps in 1498 or 1505 in the province of Coatzacoalcos. Her people were not Mexicas and her homeland was outside the jurisdiction of the Mexica tributary system. But this fact does not prevent Mexicans from condemning her as a traitor to the Mexicas and therefore to all Mexicans. Even though of noble birth, Malinalli was born under an ominous sign. Called Ce Malinalli (One, Grass of Penance), she was associated with black magic and was predicted to come into disastrous conflict with Blue Hummingbird (the ruler of the Mexicas). Malinalli probably interpreted her ominous fate not as a tragedy but rather as a sign that in joining with destructive forces, her own power and status would be greatly enhanced.

Malinalli's mother decided to give her away rather than to kill such an ill-fated child, as was the practice of the time. In addition, the mother, a widow, had remarried and wanted her newborn son to inherit all of her wealth. Malinalli was handed over to merchants, who later sold her as a slave to Mayan Indians in the present state of Tabasco. After Hernán Cortés defeated the *cacique* of Tabasco, he received twenty girls to cook for and serve the Spanish soldiers, one of whom was Malinalli. She was baptized and renamed Marina, the closest approximation to her native name.

Marina quickly proved to be an invaluable ally. She had a facility with languages—already she spoke Náhuatl and Mayan and she quickly learned Spanish. Before long, she advanced to the position of head interpreter for Cortés. Marina provided him with valuable information about the customs, habits, and ways of thinking of the Mexicas.[10] It is said that so well did Marina know Cortés's thinking and ways that she could determine what he would say before he uttered his orders. Marina warned Cortés about surprise attacks and she assumed leadership temporarily when he was wounded and incapacitated.

Mexica codices depict her as "often accompanying Cortés to the center of battle" and "carrying a shield."[11] Yet none of the codices or Spanish eyewitness accounts state that she actually killed anyone. Marina might have felt confident that her destiny in the midst of destruction would protect her from injury, so she feared no one. Her apparently "neutral" status in relation to killing might have been in keeping with the old *mociuaquetzque* tradition of ancient Indian warfare. The *mociuaquetzque* fearlessly accompanied their warrior consorts to advise, badger, incite, but never to take up weapons themselves.

Called "doña" in recognition of her noble birth and respect for her skills, Marina's many Spanish contemporaries considered her an important ally in the Conquest. The Mexicas gave Marina the reverential title of *tzin* (noble or great person) to add to the end of her Indian name—Malintzin. Because Marina always seemed to be at Cortés's side and spoke for him, the Mexicas came to call Cortés "Marina's captain or Malinche."[12]

In addition to her military and diplomatic services to Cortés, Marina became his mistress and bore him a son. Cortés had many children by Indian women and had no intention of marrying a native woman, as such a marriage would not enhance his status in the Spanish court. He married Marina to brigantine skipper Juan Jaramillo about 1524. It seems that as long as Marina was with Cortés he was successful in his endeavors. Separated from Marina, he proceeded on a disastrous expedition to Honduras.

While Cortés never married any of his Indian mistresses, he did provide land and money for their needs. Marina received in *enco-*

mienda the towns of Utlala and Tepexc near Mexico City. Cortés's treatment of Marina and other Indian women he cared for contradicts Mexican legends, which state that once her usefulness was over, Cortés threw Marina out into the streets to starve and die in squalor. In all probability, Marina died in 1529 of one of the epidemics that killed 98 percent of the native population of twenty-five million in less than one hundred years.

The historical facts also contradict Cortés's alleged actions toward their son, Martín. Martín was his favorite child, noted by the fact that he was named after Cortés's father. By papal decree, Martín was made a legitimate son. In his will, Cortés left Martín one thousand ducats a year for life. Martín became a soldier and a knight of Saint James. Yet many Mexicans prefer to call Martín a bastard child whom Cortés despised and disowned. Martín died in 1569 during the battle of Granada against the Moors. But his son, Hernán Cortés, returned to live in Mexico permanently.[13]

On May 16, 1542, seven conquistadors came together to give testimony in Marina's behalf, as the government of New Spain was disputing her role in the Conquest and attempting to take lands from her heirs. The conquistadors all "extolled the woman whose labors had been indispensable to the early conquistador successes."[14] As late as 1859, a visitor from the United States encountered in the city of Puebla a bronze equestrian statue of Doña Marina in the town square, a symbol of her as the patroness of that city.[15]

Because the Spanish Conquest was such a catastrophe for the Mexican people, the fact that Marina was among the first and foremost *soldaderas* has been obscured. The fact that no student of either Mexican or Mexican women's history has placed her within the context of army women shows just how profoundly the Conquest has scarred the Mexican consciousness. Rather than viewing Marina as a *soldadera* or a *capitana*, she continues to be condemned as "La Chingada" (the Great Whore) of a bastard race.[16] Her name, Malinche, has become synonymous with the word *traitor* among Mexicans. In fact, the belief that all things of a foreign or European nature are superior to Mexican culture is loathingly called "Malinchismo." The treatment of Marina and her son, Martín, shows that historical facts and myth are joined and share a common ground in the reconstruction of Mexican culture after independence from Spain in the nineteenth century.

Often forgotten in the vehement hatred of Marina's alliance with Cortés are the Indian women who fought against the Spaniards.

Mexica women during the Conquest supplied warriors with stones and arrows, prepared slings, and strung bows. During the last defense of Tenochtitlán and in the early stages of battle, the Mexica leader Cuáuhtemoc said to the Spaniards: "Do not talk to us anymore about peace: words are for women, arms for men."[17] When Cuáuhtemoc found that most of his male warriors were dead, he ordered "all the women of the city to take up shields and swords."[18] He told the women to climb onto the flat roofs of the houses, where they "scowled defiance and hatred on their invaders" and "rained down darts and stones" on them.[19]

While the Mexicas recognized the *auianimes* as a necessary part of their warrior society (as indicated by their participation in important ceremonies), the Spaniards attached no social value to their activities. The Spaniards viewed the *auianimes* as prostitutes and among the dregs of society. They did not understand that the role of the *auianime* went beyond just providing sex. In the battlefields, the *auianimes* were transformed into *mociuaquetzque*, the nonfighting advocates of warriors. As *mociuaquetzque*, women would taunt warriors to fight by saying, "Why are you hanging back? Have you no shame? No woman will ever paint her face for you again."[20]

The story of Érendira (the smiling one), a fearless Tarascan patriot, stands in contrast to the soldiering activities of Malinche. For all of her soldierly brilliance, Malinche still represents just one woman's reaction to the Conquest. More credit should be given to the thousands of women like Érendira who defied the Europeans. Érendira became a heroine in response to the Spanish military advances into Tarascan lands in the state of Michoacán. Much like her father, Timas, Érendira determined that the Tarascans should resist a peace treaty and alliance with the Spaniards. Her stance put her into conflict with a young warrior named Nanuma who wanted to align with the Spaniards as well as claim Érendira as his wife.

Érendira and the Tarascan king's daughters performed old rituals in which the women sang about how the independence of their people should be protected at all costs. During one of the initial battles against the Spaniards, Timas captured a white horse. He gave the horse to Érendira, who quickly became a skilled rider. Not at all happy with the defensive stance of the Tarascan people, Nanuma plotted to kill Érendira's parents, kidnap her, and join the Spaniards. While Nanuma managed to kill her parents, Érendira escaped, tracked down Nanuma, and, on her horse, trampled him to death.

Despite her heroic efforts on behalf of her people, Érendira, like Cuáuhtemoc, could not defeat the Spaniards at that time. By one account, she fled her homeland rather than submit to Spanish rule. By other accounts, she remained in Michoacán and even converted to Christianity.[21]

Unlike the state-sponsored revitalization of Cuáuhtemoc as a patriotic Mexican symbol of defiance, Indian women like Érendira are not perceived in the same heroic light. The continued focus on Malinche as a traitor and the neglect of the actions of women like Érendira is sexist and distorts the varied responses of women and their male counterparts to the Conquest.

Expansion of New Spain

Women continued to participate in the military expansion and consolidation of New Spain as a colonial empire in a variety of ways. They were either full-blooded Indian women or, increasingly, of mixed Indian, Spanish, and African ancestry. Early in the Conquest, the allegiance of many of these women was to their group of origin, but as *mestizaje* and Christianity increased, their loyalty to the original group fluctuated. Women's roles in armed groups involved family and camp duties, foraging, cooking, sewing, and helping the sick or wounded. In addition, women served the missionary and soldier/colonist expeditions as guides, interpreters, couriers, and fighters on occasion.

Indian groups like the various Chichimecs of the northern frontiers offered the Spanish-Mexicans stiff resistance. These Indians went everywhere with their womenfolk. The counsel of older Chichimeca women was highly respected, and older women could unleash tongue lashings on errant warriors. Philip Powell characterizes Chichimeca women as willing to "take up the fight, using the weapons of fallen braves."[22]

Many tribal women embraced Christianity and often offered their considerable services to missionaries and the Spanish captains. One notable example involved a Suaqui woman named Luisa and Spanish captain Diego Martínez de Hurdaide in the conquest of Sinaloa in the late 1590s and early 1600s. Much like Malinche, Luisa had once been a slave woman who converted to Christianity. Martínez de Hurdaide befriended her and she served him as an interpreter in the subduing of the Suaqui. On one occasion Luisa remained loyal to Martínez de Hurdaide while other Suaqui women attending to their captured husbands hid stones in their food bags and joined their mates in attacking the Spaniards. Over the course of many years she talked Suaqui women and men into forsaking revolt and accepting Christianity.[23] Female guides, couriers, and interpreters were often more successful in traveling through hostile lands to send or give messages to both sides. Women, unlike men, who were perceived as warriors, were considered to be "neutrals" in warfare.

Indian, Spanish, and mixed-ancestry women also formed part of expeditions into what is now the United States. Many women journeyed with Francisco Vásquez de Coronado's 1540–1542 expedition into Arizona, New Mexico, Texas, Oklahoma, and Kansas. The Indian allies who joined the three hundred Spanish Mexicans "were accompanied by their wives and children."[24] Among the colonists, three women, Señora Caballero, María Maldonado, and Francisca de Hozes, gained notice in official records. The father of borderlands historiography, Herbert E. Bolton, calls these women "soldaderas" and "Amazons." Señora Caballero is identified as the wife of soldier Lope de Caballero and "a native Indian woman, perhaps an Aztec."[25] Bolton depicts María Maldonado, wife of Juan de Paradinas, a tailor, as "an early Florence Nightingale [who] nursed sick soldiers, mended their ragged garments and was generally regarded as an angel of mercy."[26]

In a different vein, Bolton depicts Francisca de Hozes as the "talkative" and "sharp-tongued" wife of Alonso Sánchez. They had two children with them, one born somewhere on the trail. Unlike other women, who rode mules rather than horses, de Hozes rode "a horse all the way from Mexico City to the Barrancas in the Texas Panhandle and back—a good seven thousand miles."[27] A woman with a mind of her own, she complained to authorities in Mexico City about Coronado, whom she said had "mistreated and put in shackles many Spaniards who wished to stay with Fray Padilla in New Mexico rather than return to Mexico,"[28] because the journey back to the interior of Mexico was difficult.

The Opatas of Sonora had rebelled against Spanish abuses. Chief among these abuses was the practice whereby Spanish soldiers took Opata women as servants and sexual partners. Captain Alcaraz was in charge of the San Gerónimo garrison when the Opatas attacked. He was allegedly in bed with two Opata women when the battle started. The Opata women helped him into his native cotton armor (*lesquipil*) and then shot poisoned arrows between the pads of the armor, killing him.[29]

In 1598 Juan de Oñate led a group of mestizo settlers (130 women and 400 men) into the area now known as New Mexico. Two women, Luisa Robledo and Doña Eufemia, received recognition for helping to defend the fledgling settlement against hostile Indians. Robledo organized the women of the small settlement into defense units stationed on the flat rooftops of adobe houses and armed with heavy stones to throw down at all invaders. While the men were away on an expedition, Robledo and her armed women scared off "an impending attack by eastern Plains Indians."[30] The wife of the royal ensign, Francisco de Sosa Peñalosa, Doña Eufemia, gained notice from Oñate himself with her plans to help defend the settlement.

> Doña Eufemia had gathered all the women together on the housetops to aid in the defense. Doña Eufemia had stated that they would come down if the general so ordered, but that it was their desire to be permitted to aid their husbands in the defense of the capital. Don Juan was highly pleased at this display of valor coming from feminine breasts and he delegated Doña Eufemia to defend the housetops with the women. They joyfully held their posts and walked up and down the housetops with proud and martial step.[31]

Some women marched with brooms, which they used to sweep dust and dirt into the eyes of the Indians and, it was hoped, blind them.

At the same time that Spanish Mexican colonial women defended their settlements, native women were among the most verbal proponents of death to the Spanish Mexican colonists. Such was the case with the Curecho Indians, who battled against the Antonio de Espejo expedition in 1582. The Spanish Mexicans had taken a Curecho woman captive and wanted to trade her for another Indian woman who had escaped. The Curechos had, however, sent the Indian woman back to her people. They tried to dupe the Spanish Mexicans into accepting another Indian woman carefully disguised. The Curecho plan was to get their captive back in addition to an Indian female interpreter kept by the Spanish Mexicans. After a few skirmishes, all three Indian women managed to escape under a hail of arrows. The interpreter, who lured the Spanish Mexicans into the trap, later "wrestled with [a soldier] and took a knife from him and threw it to the Indians."[32]

During the Castaño de Sosa expedition of 1590–1591, Pueblo women aided in the defense of the Pecos pueblo. The Spanish Mexicans noted that all the people were armed on the adobe rooftops and on the ground. Even in the midst of battle, women carried stones to the rooftops. Lieutenant Castaño called for the Indians to give up, but instead, "an Indian woman came out from a gallery of the houses . . . and she threw some ashes at him."[33] Sometimes Indian women would hurl their *metates* (stone corn grinders) at the Spanish Mexicans. Reports from the Pueblo Revolt of 1680 state that "many Christianized Indians (as well as those who had not been converted), and particularly the women had clamored to be done with all the Spanish and put all our strength toward killing them."[34] If captured by the Spanish Mexicans, Indian women often ended up as servants and bedmates to the soldier colonists.

Women, like men, were taken as slaves to be sold on the market. Because soldiers in these far northern garrisons received so little pay, slave trading served as an alternative source of income. The Indians "de guerra" (of war) unsold on the slave market were pressed into personal service. Much like a feudal knight, the soldier of the Spanish crown would travel with his Indian servants, whom he called vassals. In 1542 the Spanish crown issued the New Laws, which forbade Indian slavery and compulsory personal service; from this time forward Indians were to be paid for their services. While these laws were well intentioned with respect to Indian slavery, they were unenforceable in New Spain and thus had little concrete meaning.

In addition to Indian slavery, large numbers of Africans were brought into Mexico as slaves to substitute for the rapidly declining Indian populace. About 150,000 Africans were sent to Mexico from 1519 to 1821. Rebellions, conspiracies, and riots against slavery occurred in 1537, 1608–1609, 1611–1612, 1664–1665, and 1735 in Mexico City and the Córdoba-Orizaba region of Veracruz.[35] The Africans revolted against harsh and repressive laws restricting their rights.

The African revolt of 1611–1612 started over the death of a female slave who had been mistreated by a Spaniard. At her funeral, about fifteen hundred people of pure or mixed African ancestry marched through Mexico City, protesting and throwing stones at the home of the accused Spaniard. The authorities immediately arrested the leaders of the protest and had them whipped and exiled outside of Mexico. The repression only served to anger the people further. They devised plans to retaliate against the Spaniards, and an uprising was planned for Easter Week, 1612.

It never happened because an Angolan woman was overheard

by two Portuguese slave traders who understood the Angolan language. They were horrified by the woman's statement that "all the Spaniards would be killed during Holy Week and that the city would then be under the control of the blacks."[36] The authorities hanged thirty-five conspirators on May 2, 1612, including seven women who were hanged and quartered in Mexico City's central plaza. Their execution indicates that, just like men, women led armed revolts and were executed.

The Spaniards also faced revolts by irate villagers and recently Christianized Indians. Staging a rebellion was often a more productive way to address and even settle grievances than to go through the lengthy process of litigation. A revolt in Santa Lucía, Oaxaca, was led by a woman named Mariana. Described as a "tall scar-faced" woman, she demanded that royal, religious, and military officials leave the village without drawing town boundary lines that villagers disputed. She severed the measuring rope and thus started a revolt. The villagers forced the officials to leave the town.[37] During the settlement of Nayarit in 1722, recently converted Indians abandoned the *rancherías* and joined a rebel band. The group attacked a party searching for mines in the area. One of the rebels who held out the longest was an "apostate female leader named Juana Burro."[38]

As the colonial settlements grew larger, so too did the presidio forces. Whereas soldiers' wives or concubines could hope to advance their status during the Conquest, the establishment of a poorly paid frontier presidio army frustrated such ambition in later generations. For example, the colonial soldier stationed in disease-ridden towns or in the far northern garrisons faced a life of "low pay and minimal rations, poor supply and equipment, lack of military training and education, too much work or not enough challenge."[39] Men with families were hard-pressed to support them on military pay. Many soldiers' wives and children resorted to begging in the streets. Some wives took in laundry and sewing to make ends meet. Despite the fact that colonial soldiers' wives began to earn money, all of it had to be spent on helping the family survive at a subsistence level.

In contrast, officers benefited from the *montepío militar* established in 1765 "as a kind of pension fund for the widows and orphans of the officers dying in the service."[40] The family received one-fourth of his annual salary at the time of his death. The fund consisted of a government subsidy of two thousand pesos and occasional supplementary treasury funds. Officers paid into the fund an unspecified monthly sum plus a 2.5 percent tax on their pay while in the corps. The combined monies produced some revenue for the royal treasury, served as a family pension fund, and offered an incentive for joining the officer corps.[41]

A colonial woman, Catalina de Erauzú (1592–1650), received immense notoriety for her military exploits and belligerent demeanor. Forced by her family to become a nun in Spain, Erauzu left the convent and became an adventuress. Disguised as a man, she became a soldier and swordswoman. She fought in Spain, Peru, and Chile until her sex was discovered (1624), at which point she was forcefully returned to Spain. On the journey back to Madrid, she wrote her autobiography, *Historia de la monja alférez*. She journeyed to Rome to petition Pope Urban VIII for permission to wear men's attire. She received a special dispensation to wear men's clothing after she discussed her exploits in the New World with the Vatican.

La Monja Alférez (the Nun Ensign) then went to Spain, where she found a protector and "succeeded in securing from the king, as a premium for her military service in America, a pension that amounted to five hundred pesos a year."[42] She collected the pension from the Royal Treasury in Mexico, where she arrived in 1630. After a few years she decided to start a mule train line of merchandise between Mexico City and Vera Cruz. Wearing her hair short, she called herself Don Antonio Erauzú and was described as dressing in men's clothing, "carrying a sword and dagger with silver trimmings, of good physique, swarthy complexion and affecting a thin mustache."[43]

Erauzú once decided to escort a young girl to a convent in Mexico City. She was challenged by an official along the way to "take off her mask" and she responded, "Neither his Majesty will know of our journey, nor will his royal service gain or lose by taking off the mask and you have nothing to gain but to get two bullets which are in this arquebuse."[44] The Nun Ensign apparently developed a deep affection for her young charge and wanted to be her protector. But the young girl met and married an hidalgo. Erauzú kept up her friendship with the woman, much to the dismay of the woman's husband, who forbade the Nun Ensign to visit his wife. In a burst of anger, she responded by challenging the husband:

> When persons of my quality enter a house, their nobility gives them assurance of receiving good treatment and I have not exceeded the limits which have been laid down by your worship, it is a disgrace

to refuse me entrance. Moreover, I have been told if I ever passed in your street you would kill me. For this, although I am a woman, apparently lacking in courage, that you may see my gallantry, I shall wait for you alone, back of San Diego from one to six.[45]

The husband answered that the Nun Ensign should leave the fighting to men and devote herself to God. Such a comment shows the constant harassment upper-class women received if they strayed from the rigid gender definitions of colonial society. The Nun Ensign, at first very angry with him, later reconciled their differences. She even aided him in a fight against three other men, "baring her sword and dagger."[46] She continued to be called "Señor Alférez" and to conduct her mule train business until she died in 1650.

The colonial period also saw the reemergence of the Earth Mother/warrior goddess cult in a Hispanic guise. The Indian Earth Mother converged with the Spanish Blessed Mother image in the cult of Our Lady of Guadalupe. By the end of the colonial period, Our Lady of Guadalupe regained her manifestation as María Insurgente, the Mexican nationalist defender. The cult started only ten years after the Conquest. In 1531 Juan Diego, a converted Indian, claimed that the Blessed Mother, Our Lady of Guadalupe, appeared to him on the site where once stood the temple dedicated to Toci and Tonantzin, ancient Mexica goddesses.

Our Lady of Guadalupe's use as a goddess of war spread initially to Europe. In the Battle of Lepanto in 1571, "Christian forces fought under the banner of Our Lady of Guadalupe when they defeated the Turks."[47] Not until the 1810 Wars of Independence did Our Lady of Guadalupe's warrior image emerge in Mexico as María Insurgente. For the insurgents fighting against Spanish colonial rule, Our Lady of Guadalupe became their "banner, their plan, their laws and institutions."[48] One man explained his participation in the revolt that Father Miguel Hidalgo started as being "in defense of the law of Our Lady of Guadalupe, just as he had previously defended the law of the Spaniards."[49] In this respect, Our Lady of Guadalupe became the catalyst of Mexican nationalism.

Octavio Paz, one of Mexico's foremost thinkers, provides a good example of the impact of Our Lady of Guadalupe/María Insurgente on the Mexican people:

Tonantzin-Guadalupe, on the other hand, conquered the heart and imagination of all. She was a true apparition, in the sense of the divine numen: a constellation of signs come from all the skies and

all the mythologies, from the Apocalypse to pre-Columbian manu-
scripts, and from Mediterranean Catholicism to the pre-Christian
Iberian world. . . . The Virgin was the standard of the Indians and
mestizos who fought in 1810 against the Spaniards, and a century
later she became the banner of the peasant armies of Zapata. She is
the object of a private, public, regional, and national cult. The feast
day of Guadalupe, December 12, is still the feast day par excel-
lence, the central date in the emotional calendar of the Mexican
people.[50]

Paz cites Our Lady of Guadalupe as the foremost religious symbol
of unification in Mexico with his references to the Mexica mother
goddess Tonantzin, Mediterranean Catholicism, and the Christian
Iberian world. He also notes the role of Our Lady of Guadalupe as a
war goddess in the rebellions of 1810 and 1910. In 1754 Pope Bene-
dict XIV authorized a special prayer and mass to be celebrated an-
nually on December 12.

Our Lady of Guadalupe served as an inspiration to Indian rebellions as well. Yaqui leader Juan Banderas had a vision of Our
Lady of Guadalupe leading his troops. As a consequence, the Yaquis drove out non-Yaquis from their lands until 1833, when the
Mexican government regained nominal control over Sonora.[51]

Besides being a symbol of prayer for male soldiers, the image
also provided legitimacy for Mexican women to combine their
traditional domestic duties with military defense. Luis González
Obregón notes this connection in his statement about women's
roles during the 1810 Wars of Independence: "During the war of
insurrection, Mexican women rescued our cities and battlefields,
like protective goddesses, announcing the genesis of our independence, reviving by their love a greater and holier love."[52] Clearly,
Mexican female fighters represented the values Our Lady of Guadalupe manifested as María Insurgente.

Forging the Mexican Nation, 1810–1821

In the nineteenth century, Mexico defeated the Spaniards, fought
the Americans and the French, and suffered internal strife from
rival political factions. Women were very much involved in all of
these struggles. The Mexican armies did not provide food for the
soldiers; rather, they were given money to pay servants to take
care of their personal needs. During the 1810 Wars of Indepen-

dence, thousands of women were mobilized for both the insurgent and the royal causes. The armies of the insurgents were called *chusmas* (mobs), whether of rural or urban origin. The rural *chusmas* came from the haciendas in the provinces; the urban *chusmas* were "improvised" armies composed of town-dwelling Indians, women, children, and old people.

The army of insurgent leader Vicente Guerrero consisted of about five hundred soldiers and twice as many auxiliaries. "The latter were characterized as chusmas (rabble). In this group were found relatives, spouses, girlfriends and other camp followers."[53] The major leader of the rebellion was Father Miguel Hidalgo y Costilla. His daughter Agustina fought with him. She joined him in all his campaigns, dressed "in the insurgent uniform of an officer."[54] Women used their involvement in war as a way to express their own "intimate suppressed rebellion which could be beautifully justified in the light of revolutionary struggle."[55]

Women may have joined the *chusmas* not only as an alternative to or an escape from restrictive Spanish Catholic mores but also as a way to serve notice to men that their "cooperation was essential to the achievement of national goals."[56] Their participation in the *chusmas*, according to Silvia Arrom, influenced the war effort and had a subtle impact on societal attitudes toward women. Women often undertook activities that their male counterparts could not do very well. They seduced soldiers into changing sides and, as servants to officers, they learned of battle plans in the making. Royalist women under the leadership of Doña Iraeta de Mier, the widow of an *audiencia* judge, started the Patriotas Marianas in 1810. The major purpose of the group centered on defending the statue of Our Lady of Remedios, the patroness of the Royal Army, from destruction by Father Hidalgo y Costilla and his rebel troops. The women's group "watched over the Virgin's statue in the Cathedral in Mexico City and sewed her image onto banners as a counter to the insurgents' banners of the Virgin of Guadalupe."[57] The group engaged in fund-raising, publishing proroyalist pamphlets, and providing money for needy families of royalist soldiers. Patriotas Marianas, which at one point numbered twenty-five hundred women, remained active for a few years after hostilities ended.

Many brave women contributed their share to the ranks of heroic revolutionaries. Antonia Nava de Catalán, known as La Generala, persuaded many lower-class women during the 1810 wars to join the insurgents as cooks and supply carriers. Much in the tradition of Queen Xochitl, she started a women's battalion. She fought with a dagger and her followers fought with sticks and rocks. After the death of her soldier husband, Nava de Catalán told Gen. José María Morelos, an insurgent leader, "Here are my four sons, three can be soldiers and the youngest can serve as a drummer boy."[58] Articles and even an illustration entitled "Call to the Women to Fight" urged women to avenge the deaths of male relatives by going to war "with cruel swords" to kill royalists.[59]

Doña Leona Vicario, like many upper-class women, received much admiration from male insurgents for her war efforts. A wealthy orphan, she escaped from a convent and gave most of her wealth to the rebel cause. She was a messenger, an arms smuggler, and a military recruiter. Jailed once, she escaped to join General Morelos in Oaxaca. Doña Leona fought, planned strategy, kept the books, supervised the care of the sick and injured, and on January 3, 1817, bore her first child in a cave hideout.[60] Her wartime efforts earned her an hacienda and three houses in Mexico City. After the war, minister of foreign relations Lucas Alamán cynically said that she joined the rebels not out of patriotic fervor but out of love for Andrés Quintana Roo. Doña Leona penned an outraged response in her husband's newspaper, *El Federalista:* "Love is not the only motive of women's actions. They are capable of all the human emotions; and the desire for the glory and liberty of their country is not foreign to them."[61] She also stated that her convictions, ideas, and actions were all her own. Alamán's views on Doña Leona were generally ignored as she was a much-honored heroine during her lifetime. Her funeral in 1842 found the nation in mourning.

Doña Leona's actions were dramatic but so too were the activities of other rebel women. They aided the cause by chiding soldiers or husbands who sided with the royalists and encouraged them to become insurgents. Some women took men to *pulquerías* (bars) and told them that joining the rebels would result in land acquisition. Women also organized networks, especially among the servants of royalist soldiers, to obtain any information useful to the rebels.[62] When arrested by the authorities, rebel women sought their release by citing pregnancy, children at home, ignorance of the wrongness of their deeds, or trickery by their rebel husbands.

Because so many women became involved in antiroyalist activities, the authorities had to impose severe sentences. A royalist judge declared that women "were one of the greatest evils we have had from the beginning of this war for on account of their sex they were the instrument of seducing all classes of persons."[63] Luisa Martínez, an insurgent from Michoacán, was executed for her war activities. Martínez considered fighting in defense of the country one of the traditional duties of Mexican women. Prior to her execution in 1817, she stated, "Why such obstinate persecution against me? I have the right to do all I can on behalf of my country, because I am a Mexican woman. I commit no wrong by my conduct, because I am fulfilling my duty."[64]

The honors given to Doña Leona and others suggest that the insurgents recognized women's efforts during the 1810 wars and were quite willing to acknowledge their importance in the creation of a new nation. But while the insurgents were more likely to honor heroines than the royalists were, the fact remains that valor and patriotism were not enough to bring about profound changes in the economic and social conditions of Mexican women.

Foreign Wars and Internal Strife, 1821–1870

Changes in the Mexican army after the Wars of Independence did not extend to the use of women as *soldaderas*. As the army became a more established part of life, so too did the presence of *soldaderas*. They participated in the wars and rebellions that plagued Mexico from 1821 to the 1870s. *Soldaderas* served as part of Gen. Antonio López Santa Anna's 1835–1838 campaign into Texas, the Mexican War of 1846–1848, the Three Years' War of 1857–1860, and the French Intervention of 1862–1867. They were camp followers to Mexican soldiers and American and French troops as well.

That Mexican women served as *soldaderas* for foreign troops is an expression of the fact that the level of nationalistic sentiment in Mexico was not yet highly developed. Many Mexican women regarded their service as *soldaderas* for domestic or foreign troops as work rather than as evidence of disloyalty. Over and over again, women used the army to gain a measure of social mobility by marrying or cohabiting with foreign soldiers. They continued to criticize Mexican officers for tactical blunders and to protest their ouster as soldiers within the ranks.

Soldaderas during the Texas campaign and Mexican War offer a unique insight into women's mixed attitudes toward constant warfare. The war that developed between Mexico and the United States had its origins in the ideology of Manifest Destiny whereby American expansionists believed that "Providence had willed them a moral mission to occupy all adjacent lands."[65] Claims by

American citizens in Mexico for damages to their property also served as a source of contention. But it was over Texas that both countries prepared for war. American and some Mexican settlers in Texas declared their independence from Mexico in 1836. Mexico refused to recognize Texan independence and considered Texas a colony in revolt. President of Mexico General Santa Anna led troops to crush the rebellion.

The *chusma* that accompanied Santa Anna's 6,019-man army consisted of "numerous children, women . . . *curanderos* (herb healers), and speculating merchants."[66] Over 1,500 women and children marched from Laredo to Béxar. Fewer than 300 women and children actually reached their destination, as many died from starvation, thirst, and the harsh environment. Mexican generals Filisola and Ramírez y Sesma both petitioned the authorities to eliminate the women from the ranks. They were informed that the women were a necessary evil because, without them, most of the men would desert.[67] Soldiers, who earned twelve and a half cents a day, knew that without the women foraging and supplying other life-supporting kinds of services, they would starve to death.

The people along the path of the march inland to Texas feared the *chusma* more than the soldiers. As one soldier observed, "Much like the locusts [they] destroy everything in their path."[68] The women of the *chusma* criticized Ramírez y Sesma for not capturing an American steamboat, the *Yellowstone*, well within Mexican territory and in full view of a superior Mexican force. Only two days before the Battle of San Jacinto on April 21, the women were separated from the men to speed up troop movements. The *chusma* women resented the separation.

An incident reported by Col. José Enrique de la Peña suggested the mixed feelings that he had about the camp followers. On September 10, 1836, de la Peña recorded that Jacinto Hernández, an artillery sergeant, had killed his wife (a *soldadera*) "for some slight provocation." De la Peña considered attacking a "weak being such as a woman" to be a "reprehensible act" on the part of a soldier.[69] As de la Peña pointed out, the dangers camp followers faced came not only from hostile enemy soldiers, but also from the soldier-husbands they served.

But violence toward women must be viewed in the context of the severe discipline imposed on Mexican soldiers. Flogging for relatively minor offenses was quite common in the Mexican army. Soldiers were punished for wearing earrings, rings, and "other types of feminine ornaments that lowered the military profession."[70] Violators were subject to one month in prison for a first offense, two months for a second, and four months for a third offense.

One of the most intriguing *soldaderas* of the Texas campaign was Panchita Alavez. Even though she was the consort of Capt. Telesforo Alavez, her actions in behalf of captured Americans were extraordinary. In the course of events leading up to the Goliad massacre, Alavez saved the lives of at least ninety-nine Americans. She was described as "small, finely proportioned, darkly radiant and obviously intelligent."[71] She often entered the barracks where the Americans were held and aided the wounded and gave them water. As the Mexican army captured various groups of Americans, Alavez, "the Angel of Goliad," talked officers out of executing many of them. She saved Col. William P. Miller and his seventy-five men, for instance. She convinced General Urrea that Santa Anna's execution order for the Goliad prisoners did not apply to them because when captured they were unarmed. At another time, Alavez argued that American doctors, wheelwrights, and blacksmiths should not be killed because the Mexican army could use their services. Her rescue of Isaac Hamilton gives an important clue to why Alavez helped the Americans. It was not because she loved Americans, was a traitor or an opportunist. She probably hated war and thought needless suffering and killing of anybody was reprehensible. When Hamilton asked how he could repay her for saving his life, she responded with, "Do a kindness in my name."[72]

The Texas campaign was just the first stage of the larger conflict between Mexicans and Americans, which resulted in the Mexican War. Chief among the causes of this war were the boundary line of Texas, U.S. recognition of Texas as a state in 1845, the American desire for California and New Mexico, and the instability of the Mexican government. U.S. strategy for winning the Mexican War relied on three armies and a naval blockade. The Army of the West took New Mexico and California; the Army of the Center drove into northern Mexico; and the Army of Occupation carried the battle to Mexico City.

Once again president of Mexico, General Santa Anna led Mexican troops against the Americans. Scotswoman Frances Calderón de la Barca observed Santa Anna's army in 1841. She noted the appearance of "various masculine women with serapes or mangas, and large straw hats tied down with colored handkerchiefs, mounted on mules or horses. . . . Various Indian women trotted on foot in the rear, carrying their husbands' boots and clothes. There was certainly no beauty amongst these feminine followers of the camp, especially among the mounted Amazons, who looked like very ugly men in a semi-female disguise."[73] Her comments reflect the rigid gender divisions that were gaining popularity among the increasingly modern and industrializing European societies. Soldiering and following armies were not proper roles for women of all groups.

The battles between the Mexican army under Gen. Pedro de Ampudia and Gen. Zachary Taylor's Army of the Center were quite fierce. The brutality of these battles and the heroism of the un-armed Mexican camp followers was described by an American soldier. Some time in September 1846, Lt. Edmund Bradford reported the actions of a camp follower named María Josefa Zozaya at the Battle of Monterrey, Nuevo León:

> Some two or three hundred yards from the fort, I saw a Mexican female carying water and food to the wounded men of both armies. I saw her lift the head of one poor fellow, give him water, and then take her handkerchief from her own head and bind up his wounds; attending one or two others in the same way, she went back for more food and water. As she was returning I heard the crack of one or two guns, and she, poor good creature fell; after a few strugles all was still—she was dead.[74]

The next day, the officer and others decided to go out on the battle-field and bury her. Much like Alavez, "the Angel of Goliad," Zozaya was named "the Maid of Monterrey." While Americans marveled at her actions, it should be pointed out that Zozaya was making a statement about the horrors of war.

In contrast, María de Jesús Dosamantes was a soldier who wanted to fight. Described as about twenty or twenty-five and dressed in a captain's uniform, her orders from General Ampudia introduced her as one who wanted "to enter the ranks of the brave to fight" and "to go to the most dangerous part of the front."[75]

Gen. Winfield Scott's Army of Occupation landed at Vera Cruz. Scott's battle plans included surrounding the city and denying women, children, and other civilians the right to leave the city. For forty-eight hours, Scott bombarded the city. The Mexican dead numbered between one thousand and fifteen hundred, most of them civilians. Fear of the ruthless tactics used by the Americans spread through Central Mexico.[76] In the town of Huamtla, Josefa Castelar, much like Molly Pitcher of the American Revolution, was credited with being the only person who remained to fire a cannon on approaching U.S. soldiers. Her bravery brought back the towns-people to fight alongside her until the Americans brought up the artillery and demolished the town.[77]

Women of all ages followed both Mexican and American troops. Upon the release of a Mexican army captured by the U.S. army at Jalapa on April 20, 1847, an American known only as "J. H. P." de-scribed the camp followers:

> The woman of sixty or more years—the mother with her infant wrapped in her rebosa—the wife . . . the youthful señorita frisking along with her lover's sombrero upon her head; even to the prat-tling girl who had followed padre and madre to the wars. . . . In addition to their bedding and wearing apparel, they pack upon their backs the food and the utensils to cook it in, and worn out as they are by the toils of the day, whilst their husbands or lover sleeps, they prepare his repast.[78]

He called the women "slaves" or "like the Indians."

His report suggests that the practice of having female camp followers was barbaric and uncivilized. Yet many American sol-diers had no problem in seeking out camp followers. Samuel E. Chamberlain, an orderly to a colonel, said that "all the Americans quartered in town, kept house with a good-looking Señorita."[79] He took as his mistress fourteen-year-old Carmeleita Veigho de Moro. He even attempted to have her hired as a laundress in the U.S. Army. But Carmeleita was already married and her husband eventually claimed her and then had her raped and killed for her transgression.[80]

American surgeon Dr. Morton was chastised because he ne-glected his patients to focus his attention on his Mexican mistress:

> The night after his [Dr. Morton's] departure from Chihuahua, two Mexican girls, . . . who had been "in keeping" before, dressed them-selves in men's clothing, shouldered muskets, and mounting horses, astride, they followed their paramours. One of these "beloved" men had sense of propriety and decency enough, to dispatch his Dulci-nea back to Chihuahua, but the other continued with Dr. Morton to Saltillo, in whose tent I frequently saw her, living with him in the most public manner![81]

Mexican women did much of the camp work for the Americans. They took in washing and sold food to the soldiers. On one occasion, food sellers had their food stands at the Jalapa camp plundered by hungry U.S. soldiers who did not have the money to pay for the goods.[82]

Internal struggles between conservative elements wanting to model Mexico after Spain and liberal forces who admired France and the United States gripped Mexico during the 1850s and 1860s. The trend toward recognizing women as patriots became more manifest in idealized eulogies. Agustina Ramírez participated in the Three Years' War between conservative and liberal elements in Mexico. Ramírez is representative of the thousands of patriotic women who joined their families in the war. Adelina Zendejas states, "They know that the country is the greatest love and has the highest duty and obligation."[83]

Born in Tequila, Jalisco, Ramírez moved in her early youth to Sinaloa. She married and had thirteen sons. Twelve of her children served as soldiers under the banner of liberal Benito Juárez. She watched her husband die in battle. Ramírez worked as a nurse and would go to the battlefields to care for any of her sons who were wounded. After battles, she would look through the battlefields for her sons. She eventually had to bury most of them.

The Third Constitutional Congress of Sinaloa gave Ramírez a modest pension of thirty pesos in recognition of her valor. The pension lasted a few years and then was stopped. Ramírez did not protest but rather earned money washing clothes in Mazatlán. She died in poverty on February 14, 1879, just a few days before the Sinaloa State Legislature was scheduled to honor her as a marvelous example of Mexican motherhood.[84]

During the 1850s, women continued to try to incorporate themselves into the armies but with little success. A female soldier, Patricia Villalobos, was ousted from the ranks during the Three Years' War. Dressed in men's garb, she served as a bugler for one general and as a lancer in another regiment. When her sex was discovered, the army cashiered her.[85]

The treatment of both Ramírez and Villalobos coincided with one of the first times that the word *soldadera* appeared in a Mexican novel. Luis G. Inclán in 1865 used the word in reference to Elisa, a lower-class woman in his novel *Astucia*. She was described as a common beggar, dressed in rags and living off soldiers until they chased her away.[86] The Mexican understanding of the word went beyond the Spanish designation of the *soldadera* as a servant of the *soldada* (soldier's pay). The *soldadera* became "the woman of the soldier," and "a woman of low status and bad manners."[87] The fact that the *soldadera* was a servant, a worker who handled the soldier's money, is obscured in the Mexicanization of the word.

As in previous wars, women aided both Mexican and foreign troops during the French Intervention. Some women fought alongside their male counterparts, while others looked at French troops as employers and marriage partners. The invasion by France started when Spain, England, and France occupied the customshouse in Vera Cruz in 1861–1862 in order to collect revenue to pay claims against Mexico. The French decided to stay in Mexico and create a new French empire in America. It was not until 1867 that the Mexicans were able to expel them.

Ignacia Reachy distinguished herself in the ranks. Reachy, who was born in Guadalajara about 1816, started a women's battalion to defend the city against the French. Col. Antonio Rojas gave her a pair of riding boots while Colonel González presented her with the uniform of a second lieutenant. She left Guadalajara to join the Army of the East. Her friend Gen. Ignacio Zaragoza put her in the Second Division under Gen. José María Arteaga. She fought well in the Battle of Acultzingo on April 28, 1862. Reachy was captured by the French while covering the retreat of General Arteaga. After a year in prison she escaped and presented herself to Arteaga for more combat duty. She became a commander of the Lancers of Jalisco and continued to fight with great valor until killed in action in 1866.[88] Reachy's story shows that there were soldiers and even some officers who welcomed women in the ranks.

Soldaderas were part of the successful Mexican forces that defeated French forces in Puebla on May 5, 1862. Every year the battle is re-created by the Zacapoaxtla Indians to commemorate the event. Yet by a strange twist of fate, only men are allowed to play all the roles, including those of the *soldaderas*. Each man "carries on his back a doll to represent a baby, and a small basket with food and water."[89] The men dressed as *soldaderas* and carrying rifles also take part in the fighting. An antecedent for this "men only" ritual battle re-creation goes back to Mexica times when the Cihuacóatl (Snake Woman) or war chief had to dress in women's clothing when entering cities recently conquered. The continuation of this ritual shows that some native groups dominated by patriarchal views still distort woman's role in warfare.

Some French camp followers called *vivandières* came with the troops to Mexico. Mexican animosity toward French military excesses extended to them. Two of them were shot near Orizaba in 1862. Their bodies were mutilated, disfigured, and stripped.[90] Mexican camp followers who followed the French troops were disparagingly known as "*zopilotes en jupons*" (vultures in petticoats). These camp followers "often relieved the soldiers of heavy loads by carrying not only their own meager belongings and perhaps, a child, but also some of the soldiers' equipment, thus increasing the latter's maneuverability."[91] In addition, camp followers frequently married French soldiers. While the French troops took the services rendered by the *soldaderas*, it should be remembered that the *soldaderas* were helped by the money they earned by "following" the French. The Mexican army realized that the services *soldaderas* gave the French were counterproductive. A song entitled "Yo soy una chinaquita" (I am half Indian/half African) was composed to encourage patriotism. A key line in the song urges women to fight the French and "defend my nation's home."[92] Afro-Mexican women were targeted because some of the French troops were from Africa.

The practice of *soldaderas* following soldiers of both native and foreign troops became entrenched in Mexico because of constant warfare from 1519 to the 1860s. Armies in Mexico did not provide their soldiers with food. *Soldaderas* filled this void and helped keep soldiers from deserting or starving. While many women were forced to become *soldaderas*, other women saw soldiers as employers. Significant numbers of women gained fame, honor, money, marriage, or a degree of independence from soldiering. Much like male soldiers, *soldaderas* were motivated by different reasons for marching with the troops. The outcome of their services also was varied. Some *soldaderas* were heroic, some were parasitical camp followers, still others were judged heroines or traitors.

3 Amazons and Wives

The women, though their job was foraging, cooking and looking after the wounded, pitched in and fought if they felt like it. If a woman's husband was killed, she could either attach herself to some other man or take over his uniform and gun herself. Almost every troop had a famous lady colonel or lady captain, a husky, earringed girl armed to the teeth and among headlong, reckless fighters one of the first.

—Anita Brenner

Brenner's description of the *soldaderas* is considered a classic and mirrors the accounts of other eyewitnesses of both government *federales* troops and rebels of the 1910 Mexican Revolution. The Mexican army became more or less a peacetime establishment during the dictatorship of Porfirio Díaz (1876–1911). Even though Díaz enacted some military reforms, elimination of the *soldaderas* was not among them.

The *soldaderas* became the semiofficial quartermaster corps for the lower ranks of Indian and poor men. Women from these groups attended to their needs as camp followers. The major role of the *soldaderas* in this peacetime army was to feed the men. The soldiers were considered day laborers and paid wages every few days or so. They would give their wages to the *soldaderas*, who would purchase food and prepare it. The *soldaderas* served the meals much like caterers who competed with each other for business. A typical *soldadera* carried a food basket complete with tablecloth, decorative plates, and, for an added touch, a vase to fill with flowers.[1]

With a limited number of revolts to put down, the peacetime army did not often go on the march. When it did the *soldaderas* who accompanied it sometimes foraged for food as well as prepared it. A European observer in 1893 noted that "they encounter little more of hardship in following the army than they do in remaining in their homes, and they are sure—as they are not sure in their homes—of a sufficient supply of food."[2] While the army was never a very attractive lifestyle for most lower-class men, the regularity of wages did attract camp followers, prostitutes, and concubines.

In 1901 women of all classes came under critical scrutiny in the sociological work of Julio Guerrero. He viewed the double standard of wife and mistress as appropriate for modern Mexico. Guerrero said that the wife "gave dignity to home and society," but "the mistress was for fun."[3] He viewed the *soldaderas* as irredeemable concubines. "They are excessively shameless," and "they use the most base language of the people."[4] Guerrero compared them with the primitive stages of civilization. He claimed that *soldaderas* tended to be mindless, because they gave "absolute fidelity" and "unconditional servitude to their soldier mates" and "acceptance of the commands" of the officers.[5]

Guerrero's beliefs reflect elitist attitudes about the character of the lower classes. His harsh depiction was meant to indict the archaic army and its practice of uprooting people and creating occupational instability. Guerrero probably wanted the army to eliminate the *soldaderas* just as "modern" countries like the United States and England had done. But his observations of the *soldaderas* are not accurate. While some *soldaderas* were docile and easily manipulated by soldiers and officers, others were not so easily cowed. *Soldaderas,* like other servants, could leave one soldier employer and work for another at will. And it was not unusual for *soldaderas* to disobey officers' orders if they seemed unduly harsh.

The events surrounding the Tomochic War of 1892–1893 in Chihuahua show *soldaderas* defying orders. In this war Indian groups like the Yaquis, Mayos, Guasaves, and Tarahumaras rose in defiance against both government and church abuses. Their heroine was Teresa Urrea, the Saint of Cabora. Urrea combined great healing abilities and criticism of the Porfirian government. She did not encourage revolution; nonetheless, she was revered as a holy person. Díaz, threatened by Urrea's large and growing following, decided to exile her to the United States. Indians calling themselves "Teresistas" protested her departure as well as other abuses. Villagers of Tomochic defeated troops in two battles. In the third battle, three hundred Tarahumara Indians fought fifteen hundred *federales*. Antonia Holguín, a sixty-eight-year-old mother whose two sons were shot dead, "picked up a rifle and fought to her own death."[6]

The *federales* systematically destroyed the town and killed as many residents as they could. A sublieutenant, Heriberto Frías, wrote a novel about his experiences, called *Tomochic*. His work, which was read by Mexico City readers, called the officer corps incompetent and accused the army of various atrocities. Frías also wrote about the *soldaderas* in the *federales* ranks. On two occasions, *soldaderas* defied orders so that they could protect soldiers. Porfirian officials suspected that Frías was the author and sought to implicate him by searching his tent for incriminating evidence. But *soldadera* Concepción Montejo, who lived with Frías on the march, alerted about the search, hid the manuscript drafts and saved Frías from a certain court martial.[7] On another occasion, *soldaderas* gave water to the soldiers on the march—in clear violation of an officer's command.[8]

Frías had mixed feelings about the *soldaderas*. He considered them among the dregs of society and womanhood, citing their "serene abnegation." But he marveled at their "unswerving heroism" in behalf of the soldiers on the march or in battle. Frías's cynical views were formed during a time of relative calm for Mexico. But his experiences on the march and in the field showed the *soldaderas* in a more positive light. The Tomochic War was a harbinger of the 1910 Revolution, during which many more Mexicans and foreign observers would witness on a larger scale the considerable soldiering abilities of the *soldaderas*.

The Mexican Revolution involved political, socioeconomic, and military struggles between various factions over control of the country. From 1909 to 1911, insurgents such as Francisco I. Madero sought to overthrow the Díaz dictatorship. With Díaz's abdication, violent internecine war took place from 1911 to 1917 over the direction of the Revolution. Contending groups such as the middle class, small farmers, and workers fought for more political rights, justice, opportunities, food, shelter, and land.

Along with the large factions of Francisco Villa, Emiliano Zapata, and Venustiano Carranza, over nineteen hundred others fought in rebel bands. The United States intervened in Mexico's civil war with the 1914 occupation of Veracruz and the 1916–1917 Pershing Expedition. The victorious Carranza and Alvaro Obregón faction consolidated its power from 1917 to 1924.[9]

The *soldaderas* participated in most of the armed groups. But the Revolution was both the best and the worst of times for the *soldaderas*. They were well represented in the one million or more killed in the civil war. At no point in Mexican history was the performance of women engaged in various kinds of armed struggle so dazzling. *Soldaderas* numbered in the thousands. But violent hostility toward army women reached a peak in 1916 when Villa ordered his soldiers to execute dozens of *soldaderas* for an attempt on his life by one of them.

As armed confrontations began to occur in different parts of Mexico after 1910, both the *federales* and rebel groups began to recruit soldiers to fight and *soldaderas* to cook and care for the men. Friedrich Katz calls the Villista army a "folk migration," and Eric Wolf says that there were "women as well as men, coronelas as well as coroneles" among the Zapatista leaders. Carleton Beals recalled talking to the wife of a follower of Zapata. He described her as "an Indian woman from the hills" who said "that for eight years the rifle lay beside her metate upon which she ground the maize for tortillas and that she had campaigned many a weary mile with her husband."[10] Rosa E. King, who lived in Morelos during the Revolution, said that the "Zapatistas were not an army—they were a people in arms."[11]

Many wives and female relatives felt duty-bound to go with their men during the Revolution. John Reed asked a *soldadera* why she was fighting for Villa. She pointed toward her man and said, "Because he is."[12] Another *soldadera* told Reed the story behind her service:

> I remember well when Filadelfo called to me one morning . . .
> "Come! we are going out to fight because the good Pancho Madero
> has been murdered this day!" We had only been loving each other
> eight months, too, and the first baby was not born . . . and I said,
> "Why must I come?" and he answered: "Shall I starve then? Who
> shall make my tortillas for me but my woman?" It took us three
> months to get north, and I was sick and the baby was born in a
> desert just like this place, and died there because we could not get
> water.[13]

Obviously, some men expected their women to accompany them out of duty to their traditional roles. Other women saw military life as a source of food. They often traded their services as *soldaderas* for a good meal. George S. Patton, Jr., a member of the 1916–1917 Pershing Expedition, remembered a woman who approached him. She said she would even live with him if he fed her.[14]

Women abandoned or abducted and raped by soldiers had little choice but to become *soldaderas*. Soldiers of most social groups procured or abducted women to serve as *soldaderas*. In 1914 the federal forces fled from Paredón, Coahuila, and left behind three hundred *soldaderas* who "within twenty-four hours . . . had all set up new households with Villa's bachelors."[15] For the most part, the *soldaderas* represented no more than 20 percent of a combined group of men and women.[16] Edith O'Shaughnessy, wife of a U.S. embassy official, recalled how federal press gangs preyed on the lower classes: "Fathers of families, only sons of widows, as well as the unattached, are enrolled besides women to cook and grind in the powder mills."[17]

The *Mexican Herald* in 1913 often reported the abduction of women from trains and villages: "More than forty women, including all of the female population of a small village within two kilometers of Jojutla were carried away by Zapatistas" (April 13). Miguel Garibay, who later moved to Manhattan, Kansas, recalled that revolutionaries, "if they wanted a woman, they carried her off by force. When they entered a town, they demanded money, women, horses and pistols."[18]

An American consular official remembered the dire situation of a woman abducted by Carrancistas in Guadalajara in 1915. The soldiers had overtaken a party of the local elite. They threatened to take all the young women and make them into *soldaderas* if they were not given ransom money. A woman, abducted days earlier from a nearby ranch, stepped forward and told the rebel in charge, "Señor Jefe, why do you not let us ugly dark colored girls go back to our homes, and take in our stead some of those pretty, white-skinned Señoritas?"[19] The soldiers took the money and kept the women. The incident suggests that probably a great many women were unwillingly pressed into service as *soldaderas*. Mother Elías de Santa Sacto, a member of the Carmelite order, recalled that in one hospital forty-five or fifty nuns who had been taken by Carrancistas were "about to become mothers."[20]

Elsie González of Newton, Kansas, remembered her grandmother's efforts to save her sixteen-year-old sister from abduction. She noted that revolutionary bands like the Dorados, Carrancistas, Colorados, and Federales "took everything, food, animals, and young women." She continued, "My grandmother in order to protect her sister, thrust a *chunde* (a large wicker basket) over her and sat on it. They could not budge her from it. There she stayed until the revolutionists left, and, in that way, probably saved the life of her sister."[21] María Cristina Flores Carlos (from Jalisco) related how a drunken soldier grabbed her in the street. He threatened her with a gun, saying he was going to take her with him. His companions tried to discourage him, saying that at age fifteen she was too young. She managed to escape, leaving him holding her rebozo. Flores Carlos said that when the revolutionaries arrived in her town she "didn't leave the house."[22]

Mollie Gossett, born in Monterrey but of Mexican and American heritage, recollected that her mother covered their heads with rags so their long hair would not be seen by Villistas. Gossett's father told the older sisters, "If some of those bandits get on this train, I'm going to have to shoot you both."[23] On many ranches and in many towns, a lookout would be posted to warn of the approach of rebel bands. José Lona of Los Angeles recalled his mother's youth on the hacienda of Peñuelas in the state of Aguascalientes: "She didn't cry, however, when one fine day Zapata's revolutionaries suddenly appeared in the doorway of their hut asking for a bite to eat. . . . Nor did she cry when her father took her and the other young girls of the hacienda into the mountains to hide them and save them from possibly being raped and/or kidnapped."[24] Juseta Sumaya, born in Cabo San Lucas, Baja California, remembered that in her town families "slept in the fields," because they feared federal soldiers "would take away the girls and abuse them."[25]

Yet some women wanted to be camp followers or to fight for idealistic or personal reasons. Contemporary observer Maud Kenyon-Kingdon emphasized the adventurous nature of the *soldaderas*. "Through the various towns and villages, lying in the direct route of the soldiers' march, there was found a class of women with the inordinate love of wanderlust; who joined the rank and file of those soldiers of misfortune and proceeded onward with them."[26] In an article entitled "Women in Men's Garb Fight with Rebels in Michoacán," the *Mexican Herald* (June 20, 1913), published in Mexico City, reported that "there were about four hundred in the band, including about twenty women, who were mounted like the men and carried guns and cartridge belts."

Mexican folklore is replete with stories of women like Carmen Serdán who fought alongside their male relatives, or like Elisa Grienssen, who fought without their help. At age twelve Grienssen became the catalyst that caused the town of Parral, Chihuahua, to throw out Pershing's troops in April 1916. From a family sympathetic to Villa, she deeply resented the Americans who had entered the town in search of him. When Grienssen discovered that the men of the town were unable or unwilling to fight the Americans, she told the municipal president, "Are there no men in Parral? If you can't get them out, we, the women, will do it."[27] She then gathered the women and children of the town and searched for guns, sticks, and rocks. She asked a man passing by to show her how to fire a rifle. Together the women and the children surrounded Maj. Frank Tompkins and ordered him to say, "Viva México, Viva Villa." Fighting broke out as the U.S. troops retreated, chased by the armed female defenders of Parral.

John Womack gives an interesting description of female rebels who fought together in Puente de Ixtla, Morelos. They were the relatives of murdered rebel men and were dedicated to avenging those murders. They were under the command of La China, a husky former tortilla maker. The *soldadera* band terrorized the Telecala district in Morelos, taking whatever they fancied.[28]

Abandoned *soldaderas* in some instances did not choose to reattach themselves to other men, but instead realigned themselves with powerful female leaders and formed their own rebel groups. Such was the case of Margarita Neri in Guerrero; Rosa Bobadilla, Viuda de Casas in Morelos; and Juana Ramona, Viuda de Flores, "the Tigress," in Sinaloa. These women distinguished themselves as soldiers and also commanded brigades of women or men.[29]

The story of Encarnación Mares ("Chenita") Cárdenas provides an example of how women could advance in rank if they proved good fighters. Mares went with her husband to fight against Victoriano Huerta in 1913. She fought so well at the Battle of Lampezos, Nuevo León, that she became a standard bearer. She began to dress in men's clothing, cut her hair short, and lowered her voice. Noted for her fearlessness, she moved from the rank of corporal to second lieutenant before fighting in the north slowed down and she left the army on March 7, 1916 (*El Nacional* [November 8, 1959]).

Col. María Quinteras de Meras presents another example of a female officer highly honored and given respect even by Pancho Villa. She enlisted in Villa's army in 1910 and by 1913 had fought in ten battles and, according to the *El Paso Morning Times* (May 7, 1914), had won "her shoulder straps" for her actions in battle. The newspaper account continues that Quinteras de Meras "shoots and throws a rope as well as any of the men in Villa's army. She wears a khaki suit and a broad brimmed Stetson. Three belts of cartridges and a Mauser rifle are thrown over her shoulders. The colonel has led many desperate charges and her followers have come to believe she is endowed with some supernatural power." Her husband served as a captain in her command and their young daughter Consuelo became the mascot for her soldiers. Colonel Quinteras de

Mares and her husband did not fight for money and even refused to take any pay from Villa.

While the *soldaderas* became a very important element in the success of various rebel groups, many officers had mixed feelings about whether they should be in the ranks or in the camps. As the Revolution progressed, these officers tried to bar women from following or fighting with the troops. Because women accompanying troops was part of Mexican military tradition, however, by the time of the Revolution, officers' efforts to modernize and make all staff and line positions "masculine" met with some hostility from soldiers. In 1912 a federal battalion actually threatened revolt when the secretary of war forbade the *soldaderas* from following the troops on a northern offensive.[30]

Soldier of fortune I. Thord-Gray noted that among the followers of Villa "the men wouldn't come without them, and it was dangerous to let them go because they might fall into the hands of the federals, while their men served with the rebels."[31] Nicolás Durán, a lieutenant under Villa, reveals why the *soldaderas* were so important to the men: "When I remember the Revolution I find very deep within me a sacred sentiment, a sort of veneration, for the Mexican woman. I will let my heart and my memory speak the words for the woman of the Revolution. She was the soul of the Revolution because she dedicated all her will to suffering."[32] Durán idealized not only the day-to-day behavior of the *soldaderas* but also their revolutionary fervor in behalf of the men. "She was an angel for the soldier; lighting his spirit so that he could reach victory because that meant the realization of the ideals of the Revolution and dignity for his sons and future generations."[33] Despite Durán's paean to *soldaderas*, few soldiers credited these women with having goals that extended beyond the hearth and the cradle.

The trains often served as the *soldaderas'* homes. Dr. Francisco Ruiz Moreno, a Villista soldier and dentist, recalled women and children riding the roofs of trains, "in box cars and also under the railroad cars on planks tied with knots."[34] Many *soldaderas* would fall to their deaths when the train would turn sharp curves or when it was blown up. On the march, Maj. Justino López Estrada, a Villista, remembered that soldiers rode on horses and women went on foot, "following or running quickly behind."[35]

The most important duty the *soldaderas* performed was finding and preparing food. Soldiers often referred to the *soldaderas'* food-gathering abilities. Maj. Adán Uro García, a Villista, said that women were very important to the Revolution as they cooked and were faithful and self-sacrificing. Villista major Constantino Caldero Vázquez recalled that *soldaderas* even "stole what they could" to feed their soldier husbands.[36] 1st Capt. Jesús Herrera Calderón, another Villista, noted that the *soldaderas* primarily took care of their husbands, but sometimes fed their husband's friends as well. Dr. Francisco Ruiz Moreno, a Villista, said that some soldiers who were alone ate with women they called mothers, who sold them food. Gen. Manuel Mendoza, a Villista, said that "with the Carrancistas the women supervised the food distribution."[37]

Soldaderas often took food, water, and ammunition to the soldiers during battle. Capt. Francisco Macías, a Villista, remembered that, while the soldiers ate, women would take up arms to defend their husbands. Such actions often ended fatally, as many women died. Lieutenant Durán said he saw thousands of dead women on the battlefields. 1st Capt. Jorge Ceceña Quiroz, a Villista, recalled *soldaderas* having babies on the road and having to take children on the march. According to Lieutenant Durán, the *soldadera* "received her newborn child in the most primitive surroundings. She would wrap him, protecting his small body with her own from the cold and dust of the roads, and then she would continue to follow the men."[38] Many *soldaderas* had children. They gave birth on the march, in the camps, and even on the battlefields. Midwives usually attended them. Some of the women who had babies in the fields died before they turned forty from reproductive ailments brought about by lack of medical aid.[39]

Soldiers described in an idealized fashion how the *soldaderas* combined their traditional roles as mother, war goddess, warrior, tribal defender, sexual companion, and domestic servant within the context of army life. Despite their sacrifices and service to their men and to revolutionary ideals, however, *soldaderas* continued to be viewed as disruptive and impediments by many army officers. Townspeople who survived their scavenging excursions viewed them negatively. Other Mexicans pejoratively judged all the *soldaderas* as little more than prostitutes who wantonly followed the soldiers. Even if soldiers raped or abducted girls or women and forced them to become *soldaderas*, the women's reputations in many villages and towns were, many times, forever tarnished.

While some soldiers praised the *soldaderas*, other veterans dismissed their efforts in military campaigns. Gen. Juan F. Azcárate said that nothing could be more false than to suggest that the insurgents had *soldaderas*. Azcárate believed that cinema created the fantasy of *soldaderas* with rebel armies. Villista sergeant Adalberto López Jara said that women stayed in their homes and only brought food to the camps. He said that it was a lie that many women involved themselves in army life. Yet he did admit that a few daring women fought in the ranks.[40]

Juan B. Rosales, another follower of Villa, said that the *soldaderas* never went with the troops who fought against Victoriano Huerta but remained exclusively with the federal army. Col. José Felipe Hernández Ortiz, another Villista officer, said that Villa's men did not have *soldaderas*, but that the followers of Carranza did. Ramón Caballero, a messenger for Zapata, contended that the chief of his group did not have *soldaderas*, but that other chiefs did. Cosme Pérez Flores, a follower of Zapata, noted that *soldaderas* followed the troops, but he was too young to have one.[41]

Villa proved the most vehement hater of the *soldaderas*. He wanted to modernize his army through changes in the mode of warfare, greater troop mobility, and a more efficient supply system. He believed that a modern army should be entirely composed of men filling all the line and staff positions. Reed, the American journalist, once asked Villa about his views of women. Villa thought that women were things to protect and to love because they could not discern between right and wrong. He acted surprised when Reed asked if women would be given the vote in the new republic. Villa had "never thought about women voting, electing a government and making laws."[42]

The legend of Pancho Villa depicts him as a very volatile personality, a military genius, and a great lover. Countless stories exist about his erotic adventures. He had at least four wives and became known as a "Napoleon of love," or a "cock of the walk." Villa constantly attempted to limit the roles women played in his army. As he built his army, women composed an important part of his forces, but as time passed, Villa deliberately excluded them. He did not like to see the *soldaderas* in the ranks or in the trenches: "General Villa several times attempted to compel the women to leave the trenches and on numerous occasions had them escorted back of the firing line to places of safety, but when the rebel chief's attention was called to some other direction on the field, they hurried to the front and continued their firing" (*El Paso Morning Times* [November 27, 1913]). Villa perceived the *soldaderas* as a burden and as hampering rapid cavalry movements. In explaining his capture of Juárez in 1913, he said, "What made the surprise attack possible, what allowed us to move freely, rapidly and silently was that we had no cavalcade, we had no camp followers."[43]

Villa cautioned his soldiers not to let women into the ranks. Some soldiers, however, initially disobeyed his orders. He made an example of one officer who had intended to take his *soldadera* into battle by shooting him and sending her back behind the lines.[44] In fact, Villa formed the Dorados (Golden Ones) as an all-male cavalry force. Female soldiers could not join and under no circumstances could a Dorado be accompanied by a *soldadera* into battle.

Because he considered women to be troublemakers, Villa tried to relieve the *soldaderas* of their function as camp followers. An American reporter noted, "Villa frowned on the 'soldadera system.' While many of these women still followed the army, their former function with Mexican troops, that of commissary and medical corps, had been to a great extent supplanted by official services."[45] Sometimes fights among the *soldaderas* would have deadly consequences for the male soldiers. In one incident, a *soldadera* picked up a bomb on the battlefield and later at camp threw it at a rival *soldadera*, blowing her up as well as "an innocent bystander, a perfectly good soldier who was needed by Villa in his business."[46] The next day, Villa had her executed with "military honors."

A possible cause for rivalry among the *soldaderas* centered on their relationships with men. Even in jest the fragility of these relationships came through. Edward Larocque Tinker caught this concern when he took pictures of the *soldaderas*. "When I aimed at one of them, a friend was sure to sneak up behind her and hold up two fingers like horns at the back of her head, as a suggestion that her man was unfaithful. This was a stock trick and they enjoyed it."[47]

The conflict between General Villa and the *soldaderas* reached a horrible climax in 1916. In that year, Villa captured the railroad station at Santa Rosalía Camargo, Chihuahua, from the Carrancistas. About eighty or ninety *soldaderas* and their children became his prisoners. A shot rang out as a bullet fired from among the *soldaderas* hit Villa's sombrero. One version of the story suggests that a *soldadera* who had lost her husband fired at Villa. According to another version, a female colonel from a rival faction, hiding among the *soldaderas*, took the opportunity to try to kill Villa. Yet another story said that the wife of the station paymaster in a moment of desperation shot at him.

Villa asked the *soldaderas* to point out the would-be killer. No one responded. According to Maj. Silvestre Cadena Jaramillo, Villa then "ordered his men to shoot the women. Nobody spoke up, they would rather die than tell who did it."[48] Going through the bodies, a soldier found a baby that still lived. Cleofas Calleros, a historian who grew up in El Paso during the Revolution, said, "One of Villa's men asked what to do about the baby and Villa said he wasn't doing any good, so to shoot him too. His orders were carried out."[49] Calleros added that Villa then "rode his horse over the dead bodies." Col. José M. Jurrieta, who saw the massacre, said, "I was reminded of Dante's Inferno by that scene, and I doubt if anyone could describe the panic and distress of those unfortunates, the tears, blood and pain of ninety women slaughtered with their Villista bullets."[50]

Some Mexican scholars cite the "cold-blooded slaughter" as evidence of a primitive, bestial mind. Such a harsh statement should be balanced with Villa's respect for bravery in battle whether on the part of men or women. He could honor a woman for courage in the battlefield and yet believe that large numbers of *soldaderas* negated camp discipline and troop mobility. Villa's violent behavior toward his real or perceived enemies is no different from that of other high-level commanders. Alvaro Obregón was accused of putting *soldaderas* and children in front of his troops to shield them and the artillery.[51]

Other officers took a more benign attitude toward the *soldaderas* on the field but not in the reorganization of the army after the Revolution. General Carranza, one of the most successful generals of the Revolution recruited many *soldaderas* into his ranks and established a "pension fund for his soldiers' widows."[52] He was diligent about reminding his field generals to implement this pension policy.

Some of Carranza's female soldiers were real fighters. Petra Ruiz, for example, joined the Carrancistas disguised as a man and used the name of Pedro. Nicknamed "Echa Balas" (Bullets), she became known as a fearless fighter with a bad temper. In one instance, soldiers were arguing over who would be the first to rape a young girl when the disguised "Pedro Ruiz" rode by and demanded her. The other soldiers were afraid of Pedro's skill with guns and knives so they let "him" take the girl. Once out of sight, Ruiz released the girl unharmed. Ruiz's battalion was part of the force that defeated the federal army in Mexico City and she was promoted to the rank of lieutenant. With hostilities winding down, Ruiz decided to leave the army. Passing in review before Carranza, she asked for her discharge and said, "I want you to know that a woman has served you as a soldier" (*El Nacional* [November 8, 1959]).

Petra Herrera wanted recognition of her considerable talents as a soldier and the right to remain in the army in active service. Like many other female soldiers, Herrera had to disguise herself as a man in order to be a line soldier and become eligible for battlefield promotions. Disguised as "Pedro Herrera," she blew up bridges and demonstrated considerable leadership skills. Once she established her reputation as a good soldier, she let everyone know she was a woman by wearing braids and soldiering under her real name. Many rival army factions sought her services. The *Mexican Herald* (January 7, 1914) reported, "Rebel leaders here were pleased to receive the first report from Peda [*sic*] Herrera, a young Mexican woman who is commanding a force of 200 men in the state of Durango. She holds rank as captain in the rebel army."

Herrera, like four hundred other women, took part in the second battle of Torreón on May 30, 1914, as part of Villa's vanguard, according to Villista Eulalio Mendoza.[53] According to Cosme Mendoza Chavira, another Villista, "she was the one who took Torreón, she turned off the lights when they entered the city."[54] Conventional histories do not mention Herrera's or women's participation in this battle. Perhaps Villa was unwilling to let it be known that woman had played such an important part in the battle. It is possible that lack of acknowledgment and failure to be promoted to a generalship motivated Herrera to form an independent brigade of female soldiers. Estimates of her army range from twenty-five to one thousand women. The size of her force could reflect her fortunes in battle, recruitment, desertions, or the biases of the soldiers who remembered her.[55]

Under Herrera's command, no man could stay the night in the camp. She stayed up at night and fired at any man who attempted to come near her sleeping soldiers. Such actions made her a star among women. One woman who knew her called her "feisty and spirited," with many followers. At the end of the hostilities, about 1917, Herrera, by now an ally of Carranza, requested not only to be recognized as a general but also to remain in active service. But Gen. Jesús Agustín Castro made her a colonel and "took the 300–400 women which she had and sent them away, because it was an army of women."[56] The female soldiers probably represented the remnants of Herrera's army at the end of the violent hostilities. Not much else is known about what happened to them.

They might well have gone their separate ways, back to their home-towns, or across the border into the United States.

The Carrancistas in Chihuahua did recruit Herrera as a spy. She worked as a bartender in Jiménez. One night a group of drunken men in the *cantina* made rude and insulting remarks to her. One of them took out a pistol and shot her three times. Maj. Dr. Cirujano José Raya Rivera, a former Villista who attended her wounds, believed that the violence against Herrera was a vendetta of some sort, because when the men learned that she still lived they returned and tried to shoot her again. According to the doctor, Herrera died of her wounds and fright.[57]

Policymakers for Carranza and Obregón also did not see any future for the *soldaderas* in the Mexican army. The second assistant to the secretary of war, Gen. Miguel Ruelas, said, "There should be organized a corps of military administration which shall eliminate from our armies the women camp followers (*soldaderas*) who, in addition to their disadvantages and the lamentable backwardness they reveal, make us the butt of all writers on this subject."[58] The army eventually cashiered the *soldaderas*. Gen. Joaquín Amaro, minister of war, banned them from all military barracks in 1925. He considered them to be "the chief cause of vice, illness, crime and disorder."[59] This shift in government policy reflects the victory of administrators and generals in the reorganization of the military, using the armies of Western countries as models. In addition, the *soldaderas* never organized into groups that agitated for incorporation into the military. The fact that thousands of *soldaderas* had been killed during the Revolution had no bearing on the decision to eliminate them from the army.

Although the *soldaderas* were banished from the federal barracks, women still followed troops during the Cristero Rebellion of 1926–1929 and an uprising of army officers in 1929. Waged by fanatical Catholics, the Cristero Rebellion emerged out of Jalisco in response to what they considered the antireligious sentiments of the government in Mexico City. The Cristeros numbered about forty-five hundred, according to government estimates, with about one-third of them in Jalisco. Women belonged to the Feminine Brigades of Saint Joan of Arc. Founded in June 1926, in Guadalajara, Jalisco, they operated in squadrons to "obtain ammunition in various ways, including manufacturing it themselves and distributing it through a complex network of supply routes."[60] The Feminine Brigades, considered to be very independent, nonetheless were credited by field commanders as a major reason "for the rebellion's success in sustaining itself."[61]

Enrique Gorostieta y Velarde, the leader of the National League for Religious Defense (Liga Nacional Defensora de la Libertad Religiosa—LNDLR), the main coordinating Cristero group, had to smooth out relations with the Feminine Brigades. By 1928 the Brigades had grown in numbers and efficiency and had become an important part of the Cristero effort. The Brigades at this point obeyed the LNDLR leadership only occasionally. The feud between the Brigades and the LNDLR resulted in a "serious decrease in the flow of ammunition."[62] Eventually, the friction was resolved and the Brigades increased the supply of ammunition to the field soldiers. With the decline of the rebellion and demobilization, the Feminine Brigades dissolved.

The 1929 officers' revolt involved nearly a third of the officers and 30,000 troops. Large numbers of *soldaderas* initially accompanied these rebellious troops. But at one point, the rebels abandoned over 350 *soldaderas* and their children in order to achieve greater mobility. Federal troops under Pres. Plutarco Elías Calles also had *soldaderas*, but he ordered the troops to proceed to the North without the *soldaderas* for faster movement by train. He succeeded in detaching the men from the *soldaderas* because the government provided for the soldiers' food and personal needs.[63] The revolt ended when most of the major leaders escaped into the United States in 1929.

After the fighting stopped, the army and the government continued their indifference to female veterans. When it came to pensions, the government appeared stingy, ignoring the terrible living conditions suffered by the families of veterans. Female soldiers had a better chance of securing veterans' pensions than the camp followers. They could ask their superior officers to verify their armed participation in battle, thus proving their eligibility, but the pensions were often so minuscule as to have little consequence.

The case of a well-known female soldier, Valentina Ramírez, typifies the fate of many *soldaderas* who survived the Revolution. Ramírez fought at the side of Gen. Ramón F. Iturbide from 1917 to 1920 and is considered to be the inspiration for the classic revolutionary *corrido* "La Valentina." She received a pension, but it was so small that she could barely buy food. As a result, she had to live in great misery in the slums of Navolato, Sinaloa.[64]

Part of the reorganization of the army in Mexico included a re-emphasis on the *soldaderas* as primarily wives and other female relatives. This changed the traditional perception of them as servants to their soldier employers. Thus the work they did in the camps became equated with the housework that all women did for their husbands and families without compensation. In general, *soldaderas* who labored in the camps were not considered eligible for veterans' benefits even if they did engage in occasional combat. Only the female relatives of Carranza's soldiers received small pensions as relatives of dead soldiers.

Soldaderas from other military factions also needed pensions. In 1935 Ana María Zapata, the daughter of Emiliano Zapata, enlisted the aid of Pres. Lázaro Cárdenas to organize the Unión de Mujeres Revolucionarias (Union of Female Revolutionaries). La Unión pressed for pensions for the widows, daughters, and sisters of dead revolutionaries. At one point, over eight thousand women from Morelos, Oaxaca, Puebla, Guerrero, and Hidalgo joined the group. The organization obtained many pensions and entered politics and supported the candidacy of Gen. Juan Andrew Almazán. He lost the election to Manuel Avila Camacho, however, and the power of La Unión waned.[65]

President Avila Camacho further undercut the power of La Unión in 1941 by creating a committee to better the lives of soldiers' wives and families. Lucina Villarreal, professor of fiscal education and small industries, headed the committee. Named "Jefa de la Sección Feminil" (chief of the Women's Section), she encouraged the *soldaderas* to form consumer cooperatives within all the corporate military zones. As a social worker, Villarreal rewrote army regulations to guarantee family access to the paymaster, travel arrangements, and housing.[66]

It was during the Porfirian peacetime army that the *soldaderas* became solidly entrenched in the Mexican military establishment. The widespread and extremely bloody Revolution saw many women willingly and unwillingly serve as *soldaderas*. While some female soldiers gained veterans' pensions based on their war activities, most camp followers did not. It took tremendous political activism even to gain pensions as relatives of deceased male veterans.

While *soldaderas* numbered in the thousands, there was not much national debate over changing Mexican society to encompass an army in which men and women were treated equally as soldiers. The army in this respect mirrored the larger society in which women did not have the vote and faced many restrictions based on gender bias. By the 1930s *soldaderas* had been redesignated strictly as female relatives of soldiers. Subsequent social discourse about equality between men and women in the military precludes any future use of the word *soldadera*. Women who serve in the ranks of the Mexican armed forces are now officially called *soldadas*.

In the Thick of the Fray 4

The army is of both sexes, and one cannot tell who is of more value—
the men or the women.

—*Vicente Blasco Ibáñez*

In 1914 *soldaderas* from both federal and rebel armies in Chihuahua complicated an already delicate international incident between Mexico and the United States. Scattered fragments of Gen.
Salvador Mercado's *federales* crossed the Rio Grande in retreat
from constitutionalist forces under Francisco Villa. The army was
composed of 3,557 officers and men, 1,256 *soldaderas*, and 554
children.

The captured army was interned in U.S. forts from January to
September 1914 under an 1899 convention governing the crossing
of belligerent troops into a neutral country. Initially jailed at Fort
Bliss, Texas, the prisoners were moved inland to Fort Wingate,
New Mexico, in May, shortly after the U.S. invasion of Veracruz.
The detainment of the federal army was part of U.S. efforts to oust
Pres. Victoriano Huerta from office by depriving him of soldiers to
squelch the rebels in Chihuahua. The loss of this army ended the
federales' control of Chihuahua and marked "the beginning of the
end" for Huerta's rule in Mexico.[1]

The imprisonment of the *federales*, complete with the *soldaderas* and their children, led to some of the "most prolific sources
of trouble" and presented "many knotty problems to those in
charge," according to Capt. George H. Estes, the officer in charge of
the Fort Wingate camp.[2] U.S. Army officials had difficulty in dealing with an army where women were housed in the barracks with
the men and played key roles in terms of spying, gun running,

fighting, foraging, cooking, medical aid, and dozens of other kinds of services.

Although the U.S. Army would have liked to intern the men only, they had to allow the women to stay in the camps because to do otherwise would have resulted in revolt by the Mexican soldiers. While the U.S. military command recognized this reality about the Mexican army, many American civilians did not. Diatribes against the *soldaderas*, often voiced by American middle-class women, lambasted the presence of the *soldaderas* in the camps as charity and quite unnecessary.

Many of the events surrounding the internment of the *federales* are well documented in histories dealing with the revolution in Chihuahua, with rivalries between key male personalities, with battles fought by the different factions, and with U.S. involvement. But the actions of the *soldaderas* in both federal and rebel armies are obscured. In similar fashion, the nuts and bolts of the internment camp experience have also been largely overlooked by scholars. By incorporating the *soldaderas* into the chain of events that took place in Chihuahua and the United States, insights can be gained into the functioning of the Mexican army on the march, in battle, and in camp situations.

While General Mercado of the federal army and General Villa of the rebel army both hated to see *soldaderas* among their forces, they could do little to prevent women from soldiering or following the troops. In fact, from November 1913 to January 1914, women were part of the battles, retreats, and strategy both generals used against each other.

As already mentioned, Villa thought the *soldaderas* were a burden and hampered rapid cavalry movements. Several times during the battles of Tierra Blanca, Santa Rosalía, and Ciudad Chihuahua, Villa ordered the *soldaderas* to leave the trenches and even on occasion had them escorted to the rear. But when his presence was called for at some other part of the battlefield, the *soldaderas* "hurried back to the front and continued their firing" (*El Paso Morning Times* [November 27, 1913]).

Villa's foe, General Mercado, also had negative views of the *soldaderas*. He had been made commander of the Division of the North in Chihuahua in 1912. He was in charge of stamping out the rebellion against President Huerta, which had arisen after the murder of Madero. John Reed, an American journalist, described Mercado as a "pathetic, worried and undecided little man."[3] There was much professional jealousy between *federales* regulars and irregulars.

Rival officers from the irregulars, especially Pascual Orozco and José Inés Salazar, considered Mercado a coward who retreated from battles at Tierra Blanca and Ciudad Chihuahua. In fact, Mercado's nickname was "the evacuator." The bickering between the regulars and the irregulars "sometimes undermined the effectiveness of the federal war machine."[4]

A gray-haired Indian *soldadera* from San Luis Potosí said that Mercado was "an old fool" who constantly "grumbled" about the presence of the *soldaderas*. Describing herself as a woman who refused to be "put upon," she remembered that when Mercado evacuated Ciudad Chihuahua and "ran away" to Ojinaga near the U.S. border, she decided to leave the federal army and attach herself to "a nice, handsome young fellow" in the Maderista army.[5]

Mercado left Ciudad Chihuahua for Ojinaga with nine thousand to ten thousand soldiers, *soldaderas*, Mexican and American civilians on November 29, 1913. This evacuation shocked the irregulars and the townspeople of Chihuahua because it meant that Villa would gain control of most of the state. In the midst of the trek to Ojinaga a reporter for the *El Paso Morning Times* (December 5, 1913) speculated that the federal forces were keeping the women and children as hostages against attack by General Villa's troops. Villa agreed, saying that he would not pursue the *federales* because that might endanger the lives of the women and children. The slow march to Ojinaga took fifteen days in the Chihuahuan desert and resulted in the deaths of many.[6]

The *federales* entrenched themselves at Ojinaga while a vacillating Mercado pondered his next move. Rebel forces under Pánfilo Natera staged attacks against the *federales* shortly thereafter. During the lull between skirmishes, the *federales'* *soldaderas* often visited the trenches, and sometimes they were caught in the resumption of action. A rebel attack on January 5 came while *federales* and their wives were huddled together behind the breastworks eating and smoking during a noon siesta. After one skirmish, litter carriers took from the battlefield the corpse of a woman who had been found dead in the trenches with her infant still in her arms. On another occasion, a *soldadera* gave birth to a boy in the trenches. She had to be carried away from the battle lines and across the Rio Grande for medical aid at Presidio (*New York Times* [January 2, 5, 13, 1914]).

After the engagements, *soldaderas* usually went through the battlefields looking for wounded soldiers as well as scavenging for usable items. They found a seriously wounded twenty-year-old soldier still alive even after a "mercy shot" to the head. The *sol-daderas* took him to the makeshift hospital at Presidio where he made an astonishing recovery (*El Paso Morning Times* [February 3, 1914]). The *soldaderas* also performed burial ceremonies for fallen soldiers. They would erect crosses made from stones or cactus thorns (*New York Times* [January 13, 1914]).

While the *federales* were at Ojinaga, U.S. immigration officials gave the *soldaderas* permission to cross the border to purchase supplies at Presidio. But the Americans soon discovered that the *soldaderas* were also transporting ammunition and guns. *Federales' soldaderas* at Ojinaga volunteered to bring ammunition from Presidio whenever the supplies ran low. They would go to a place in the mountains close to Presidio where *federales* arms agents had huge quantities of ammunition stored. According to one report, the women made small belts that dropped near the knees. In these belts and pockets, they carried several hundred rounds of ammunition. In fact, the women were said to carry from seventy-five to one hundred pounds in this fashion. The *soldaderas* made "frequent" trips to Presidio and "kept the garrison well supplied during the siege of Ojinaga until Mercado gave the order to retreat" (*El Paso Morning Times* [January 24, 1913]).

U.S. Army and immigration officials discovered that women who were not checked by border guards proved to be the most successful of all Mexican gun and ammunition smugglers. Mexican women were thought to have taken "millions of rounds of ammunition, countless rifles, machine guns and many cannon over the boundary line" (*El Paso Morning Times* [January 24, 1913]). The United States finally put a dent into the practice by having female inspectors check all Mexican women who crossed the border. Women were sometimes taken off buses and trolley cars near the border at El Paso under suspicion of ammunition and gun running (*El Paso Morning Times* [May 6, 1914]).

Despite the fact that his *federales* had sufficient supplies to continue to hold out at Ojinaga, Mercado decided to retreat across the border. His decision was probably influenced by the approach of Villa, who had decided to take command of the rebel force. In addition, in the past, when a Mexican army fled into the United States, the American army would disarm them and let them slip back into Mexico at a safer place. The *federales* could not have anticipated that the Americans would change this practice and detain them indefinitely.

In speaking to the American press, Mercado kept his real reasons for the retreat secret. Instead, he said he ordered the evacuation of his army on January 10, 1914, because he feared that the unarmed *soldaderas* and children would have been killed in battle. Mercado also mentioned, almost as an afterthought, that many soldiers and officers believed that if captured by the rebels they would be executed (*Los Angeles Times* [January 12, 1914]; *Mexican Herald* [January 12, 1914]).

The *soldaderas* intermingled with the soldiers during the retreat, which took place in the moonlight on January 10. They walked singly, carrying babies on their backs in *rebozos,* or on burros loaded with children or family belongings. As the retreat progressed, some soldiers panicked and knocked over women and children as they rushed across the Rio Grande. A U.S. Army observer noticed a crying *soldadera* on a horse riding back along the column calling for her husband. They had become separated and she feared that he had been killed or had gone back to Ojinaga.[7]

Once across the border, the federal army was placed into a vast corral by the American soldiers. No one was allowed to leave. This caused the *soldaderas* great concern because some had lost their children in the chaos and wanted to find them. They had to wait until morning, however. Counting the children of the *soldaderas* proved to be an embarrassing problem for the American soldiers. An initial count listed only a few. The soldiers doing the counting complained that it was necessary to search every woman closely to detect the presence of children. Most of the five hundred children eventually counted were nursing or strapped to the mother's body in a *rebozo.*[8]

After the first night in the camp at Presidio, the *soldaderas* were reunited with their families. The camp was described as an army that dissolved at nighttime as the soldiers joined their family groups. A custom that impressed American observers was the appearance of small niches, hollowed out of the dirt walls of the arroyo, that featured religious and family articles, pictures, and lighted candles.[9] Ernest P. Bicknell, a Red Cross official, found the night camp, with the flickering candles and people praying at their homemade altars, a very moving experience.

Yet the camp was not as peaceful as the Americans thought, primarily because not all the female soldiers had surrendered. Many had not retreated with Mercado. They had, in fact, evaded capture and refused to lay down their arms as the camp followers had done. Such was the case with Capt. Clara Ramos. She appeared among the *federales* in the Presidio camp. A federal officer, Lt. Col.

Ernesto Silva, was sleeping when he was awakened by La Capitana wearing an officer's long campaign overcoat. She informed Silva that she commanded a company of irregulars loyal to Orozco, a rival of Mercado. With her troop she had fought in all the campaigns against Madero and had remained in the border area near Ojinaga until Mercado had retreated. She then decided to infiltrate the Presidio camp and help *federales* escape. La Capitana explained that as the *federales* fled across the Rio Grande, many had dropped their Mausers and ammunition. She had collected and hidden them in a safe place. She urged Silva to gather other soldiers and follow her back to Mexico. Silva and about seventy others agreed to her plan and followed her to Ojinaga. They evaded both U.S. troops and Villa's rebels and successfully reached Mexico City (*Mexican Herald* [February 6, 1914]).

Immigration inspector George Harris depicted the *soldaderas* as almost always engaged in the preparation of food by day. He admired the skill they showed in making use of "whatever chance, charity or mayhap their own enterprise threw in their way."[10] He noticed *soldaderas* laughing while making the food, but also met a *soldadera* who told him in disgust that all the soldiers thought about was war and fighting.

U.S. army doctor Louis C. Duncan noted in the Presidio day camp that while women seemed out of place in an army, a wounded Mexican soldier was "lucky" if he had a *soldadera* with him. The *soldadera* "looked out for his belongings, took care of him, procured his food and cooked it, washed his clothes and in fact did everything she could" for him.[11]

The U.S. Army had difficulty in providing food and other supplies for the captured army at Presidio. Instead of letting the federal army recross the border at a safe place, the U.S. high command decided to march the army inland to Marfa, Texas, a distance of sixty-seven miles. From there, the *federales* were to be sent by train to Fort Bliss in El Paso. Pres. Woodrow Wilson was demanding that Huerta either resign from office or declare himself ineligible for the presidency of Mexico in new elections. Criticism of Wilson's policy was offered by a civilian concerned about the poor in the United States. W. H. Spaulding of Flagstaff, Arizona, sent a telegram to L. H. Garrison, secretary of war, asking whether "American citizens destitute and unemployed [could] obtain food and lodging at the Mexican refugee camp."[12]

The Americans thought the journey would greatly tax the *soldaderas*. General Mercado assured them that the women could keep up. He said that "the women would not impede the progress of the column, as they were accustomed to outdoor life and capable of enduring fatigue" (*New York Times* [January 19, 1914]).

The *soldaderas*, covered by vivid green, blue, red, or yellow blankets, were considered the best marchers. There were instances of women yielding their place on horses or burros to other women or to men who were tired. It was out of a sense of chivalry that the U.S. soldiers had ordered the women to ride the horses. This practice was not followed by the Mexican army; customarily, a soldier rode the horse while a *soldadera* walked (*New York Times* [January 19, 1914]).

On the march to Marfa, the *soldaderas* carried their usual load— small children, pots, pans, kettles, and bedding. About twelve miles from Presidio, a *soldadera* gave birth to twins; an older woman served as the midwife. One child lived but the other died. Another *soldadera* gave birth to a stillborn baby, which was buried along the roadside. In another instance, a *soldadera* gave birth to a girl. The news became a topic of lively conversation among the Mexican army. Often after a child was born, the entire company would gather for a baptism ceremony (*The Outlook* [January 31, 1914]; *El Paso Morning Times* [January 21, 1914]).

The *soldaderas* took great care to keep their hogs, burros, chickens, and firewood in place. Many *soldaderas* had chickens with them and carefully guarded them during the battles at Ciudad Chihuahua and Ojinaga and the march to Marfa. One *soldadera* refused to march until one of the soldiers picked up a bundle of ironwood sticks that had fallen from a burro. Even though assured that there was plenty of firewood in the Marfa camp, the *soldadera* would not move until the bundle was strapped to the pack saddle (*The Outlook* [January 31, 1914]; *El Paso Morning Times* [January 21, 1914]; *Los Angeles Times* [January 19, 1914]).

The question of what to do with the *soldaderas* became a topic of concern for the U.S. Army high command. In correspondence between army officers, Gen. Tasker Bliss reported that "the wives and children form part of a Mexican command and do the soldiers' cooking."[13] He thought that it would be "very unwise" to separate them. Maj. Gen. and Chief of Staff Leonard Wood concurred in a return telegram that "all prisoners and refugees of strictly military character including women and children should be taken to Fort Bliss and detained there."[14]

While the U.S. high command might well have decided to detain the *soldaderas* and their children to prevent a possible uprising by the federal troops, that was not the rationale that Gen. Hugh Scott, commanding officer at Fort Bliss, presented to the El Paso City Council. He said that taking care of the wives and children was merely an act of humanity. Captain Estes, in charge of the Mexican camp, added that the "women and children were held solely as an act of charity," and that "such action was desired by all concerned."[15]

After the federal army arrived at Marfa, they were loaded on six trains and sent to Fort Bliss. The U.S. Army cleared the ground of the twenty-seven-acre campsite and installed water pipes and electric lights. The *soldaderas* put up the tents and cleared the streets of sand burrs. A newspaper reporter subjectively added that, aside from fighting once in a while, *federales* basically smoked cigarettes the rest of the time. The reporter likened the Mexican camp to a picnic with children, dogs, and the aroma of coffee and tortillas in the air (*El Paso Morning Times* [January 22, 1914]).

In the Fort Bliss camp, the U.S. Army decided to make a more accurate count of the *soldaderas*. They divided them into two groups. The larger group was "attached" to male soldiers, while a smaller group of 138 women and 72 children was designated as "unattached women and children." This group, housed in a separate section of the camp, consisted of widows, servants, and young male camp followers. The U.S. Army wanted to release the unattached camp followers to the Mexican consul in El Paso, but the plan never went into effect. Subsequent plans to get rid of these camp followers also failed. The women could not pass strict immigration laws for release, and then disease among the prisoners, especially smallpox and typhoid, made release impossible. Yet at all times during the detainment of the *federales*, any woman could leave on the proviso that she never return or if she was able to comply with U.S. immigration rules.[16]

The problem was not only that few *soldaderas* left the camps voluntarily, but that many female relatives of soldiers wanted to live in the camps. When the wives of several high-placed officers learned that their husbands had been interned at Fort Bliss, they left their homes in Mexico to join them. Mrs. Francisco Castro, her three sons and daughter left Ciudad Chihuahua to join General Castro, the second-in-command of the federal army. Mrs. José Inez Salazar also gained permission to join her husband at the camp. She had been living in El Paso since February 1913, and her four children were said to be attending public schools in El Paso. Army officials received many applications from other female relatives of the soldiers asking permission to live with their men.[17]

Two women, Carmen Parra y Alanis and Luisa García, appeared in El Paso on March 4, 1914, with the purpose of visiting Col. Lásaro Alanis, the husband of Carmen Parra and supposedly a prisoner at Fort Bliss. The two women described themselves as holding commissions as *federales* irregulars. They had been at the Battle of Ojinaga, but unlike the regular forces under Mercado, they had guided their soldiers to Saltillo, Coahuila. The presence of Parra searching for her husband leads to several questions, especially as her husband was not listed as being a prisoner. Either he was there under an assumed name, which is unlikely, or Parra ("La Coronela") was there as a messenger and a spy (*El Paso Morning Times* [February 1, 1913; March 5, 1914]).

The fact that she was not immediately arrested shows that the U.S. Army did not think that female soldiers were as dangerous as male soldiers. Gen. José Inés Salazar, in contrast, was at Ojinaga, evaded capture, and was eventually captured on U.S. soil. Both Salazar and Parra had long and impressive careers as revolutionaries.[18] Yet Parra was never arrested by U.S. authorities for neutrality violations, as Salazar was when he entered the United States, in spite of the fact that in May 1911, she and her men briefly captured Juárez and shot up the town. She then participated in battles at Conejo, Rellano, La Cruz, and Bachimba in 1912 and commanded the rear guard in the recapture of Juárez by Red Flaggers allied with the *federales*.[19]

As American experience with the role of women soldiers in the rebel bands grew, the policy was changed. For example, two women, Mrs. Castillo and Cimona Gallegos, who accompanied Máximo Castillo, another prominent escapee from Ojinaga, were arrested in the United States and placed in the internment camp. Castillo and his group had not fled across the border with Mercado's forces but had stayed in Chihuahua and continued to harass Villa's forces. His rebel band was implicated in the disaster at the Cumbre Tunnel when the rebels set fire to a passenger train and killed fifty people, some of them Americans. Whenever the rebel band was sighted, reference was usually made to the presence of these two women. In fact, Mrs. Castillo had given the *El Paso Morning Times* an interview the year previously (February 19, 1914) stating that she was a messenger and go-between for her husband and General Huerta. Cimona Gallegos, a twenty-year-old woman, was one of the few *soldaderas* who was named in U.S. records.[20]

The U.S. Army had a major problem with the *soldaderas* over who would cook the soldiers' food. The army thought that all the Mexicans should be fed like everyone else, at mess tents with army cooks making the food. Forty army mess tents with forty cooks were set up. While this arrangement was practical for a modern army, it was unacceptable to the *federales*. They were used to eating only Mexican food cooked by the *soldaderas*. Rather than eat the U.S. rations, the majority of the prisoners stopped eating. Peter B. Kyne, a reporter for *Collier's Magazine*, noted that "some ate the army ration, some starved, none liked it and the camp on the whole languished gastronomically."[21] After calling for a meeting, U.S. Army officials decided that daily rations would be issued to the heads of families. The *soldaderas* took over the cooking and set up adobe bake ovens in front of each family tent. The army also purchased thirty-six hand-powered corn grinders and placed eighteen on each side of the camp. The grinders were in operation from morning to night.[22]

The appeal for clothing for the *soldaderas* drew heavy criticism from the larger American community in El Paso. It was easier to provide the male soldiers with old army blankets, obsolete fatigue clothing, campaign hats and shoes from the various U.S. arsenals. In addition, the Mexican consul in El Paso, Miguel E. Diebold, arranged for additional clothing for the officers and men. But he could not offer any help in providing clothing for the *soldaderas* and the children, "who were in more need of attention than the men."[23] Villa heard about the plight of the *soldaderas* and sent the women "over 1,000 pesos in gold."[24] But the *soldaderas* still were in need. Lack of adequate clothing was cited as the cause of death for a child born in the camp. The child died "during the night from exposure and lack of proper clothing as there was no layette and only an old soiled shawl to wrap the child" (*Los Angeles Times* [January 25, 1914]).

The Associated Press and local El Paso newspapers picked up the story and carried an appeal for women's and children's clothing. As a result, clothing poured into the camp from individuals and charitable societies from all sections of the United States. But some El Paso residents took exception to the appeal for clothing. Julia Sharp, society editor for the *El Paso Morning Times*, was the most hostile. She said that Americans should not feel sorry for the *soldaderas.* "They enjoy the fact that they can straggle on behind the guns. What would be death to an American woman is an appetizer to the class of Mexican woman found at Ft. Bliss" (January 23, February 4, 1914). Sharp cautioned her readers that clothing and money given to the *federales* prisoners should instead go to the "worthy poor" of El Paso.

Sharp's articles stirred up a minor debate among the newspaper's readers. One letter writer said that Americans should be charitable toward all, while two other readers said generosity to the *federales* prisoners was a misuse of charity. Mrs. J. C. Jarvis remarked that if rich Mexicans in El Paso did not give the prisoners money, the internees should learn to do without help. An El Pasoan calling himself "O" feared that the *federales* would foment trouble and Villa's forces would retaliate against El Paso (*El Paso Morning Times* [February 7, 8, 1914]). In an effort to quell the debate, the U.S. Army thought it more prudent to secure appropriations from Congress totaling $4,621.75.[25]

The debate in the newspapers over clothing for the *soldaderas* grew into criticism over the extraordinary means taken by the U.S. Army to keep the Mexicans in captivity. The camp itself was viewed as an indictment against President Wilson. *Collier's Magazine,* noted for its anti-Wilson sentiments, published a full-page editorial cartoon satirizing the camp at Fort Bliss.

The possibility of a war spreading along the border after the U.S. occupation of Veracruz in April 1914 frightened many El Paso residents, especially with so many Mexican army prisoners housed at Fort Bliss. The escape of some Mexican soldiers from the camp also fed fears that army renegades would cause serious trouble in El Paso. Nor did the rival rebel factions in Mexico like so many *federales* held at Fort Bliss. They might escape and start a counterrevolution against the rebels. As a consequence, the federal army was transferred inland to Fort Wingate, New Mexico, during May 1914. Located twenty-five miles from Gallup, Fort Wingate is situated in the middle of the Navaho and Zuni reservations (*Collier's Magazine* [August 1, 1914], p. 20).

Before the transfer to Fort Wingate, medical examinations were given to all the prisoners. It was discovered that thirty-five boys listed as camp followers had to be reclassified as girls.[26] U.S. records note the reclassification but do not speculate on the reasons why thirty-five girls were passing as boys. It may well be that the girls' parents or guardians had dressed them as boys and upon their death or disappearance, the girls had kept up the disguise. These young girls might also have dressed like boys to protect themselves from soldiers looking for women.

At the Fort Wingate camp, *soldaderas* helped the U.S. Army prevent escapes. Even at the Fort Bliss camp, *soldaderas* had informed on men trying to escape through tunnels. At Fort Wingate, a *soldadera* described as a "jealous" woman revealed the existence of two escape tunnels. The tunnels were discovered and measures taken to stop their construction. General Mercado accused a sentry of the 20th battalion of arbitrarily shooting three refugees, one of whom was a woman. After the discovery of the tunnels and the shootings no one else escaped from Fort Wingate.[27]

The *soldaderas* may have informed on the men because of revenge or a lack of loyalty to the *federales'* cause. As noted earlier, often women became *soldaderas* because they had no choice. It was either follow the army, starve, or get raped. On the other hand, the *soldadera* who Mercado said was shot might be representative of women who were openly critical of the continued imprisonment of the soldiers.

Captain Estes, the officer in command of the Fort Wingate camp, expressed contradictory sentiments about the morality of the *soldaderas*. He reported that marital relations tended to be very lax. He described with disgust the fact that very few of the *soldaderas* were legally married to the soldiers they accompanied. Then he admitted that the *soldaderas* did seem to have lived happily and faithfully with their "so-called" husbands for many years. He seemed surprised that *soldaderas* would leave one man for another, especially if the latter had more money or possessions.[28]

A permanent detention area was established for *soldaderas* who engaged in repeated acts of infidelity or who appeared incorrigible. On May 23 Estes asked his superiors that Guadalupe Ramírez, a prostitute, be "either expelled from camp or subjected to disciplinary confinement."[29] Estes chose women of "good character" to work for pay as domestic servants, laundresses, and seamstresses for American soldiers and their families.

While the U.S. Army did not bother to provide much personal information about living *soldaderas*, it did list the names and ages of women who died. Fourteen *soldaderas* died during the entire detainment, four from gastroenteritis, four from tuberculosis, two from heart disease, one from cancer, one from peritonitis, one from mitral stenosis, and one from chronic dysentery.[30] When the *soldaderas* died, the Mexican consul was informed and their remains were either returned to Juárez or buried at the Fort Wingate cemetery.

Notice of the deaths of three *soldaderas* was sent to the Spanish consul, suggesting that these women held Spanish citizenship in Mexico. During the Revolution, Spanish citizens were often murdered or treated very badly by Mexican rebels. Since the Conquest, many Spaniards had become identified with oppressive and ruthless elements in Mexican society. Villa, who hated Spaniards and executed them at every opportunity, warned them to leave Ciudad Chihuahua with Mercado before he took the city or face the consequences. It might well have been that these three Spanish women and their male relatives joined the *federales* for protection against the rebels.[31] Twenty-eight children were born during the detainment. Surprisingly, the U.S. Army listed only the names of the soldier fathers and not the names of the *soldaderas* who bore them. Only the names of the fathers were listed for the nine stillbirths that occurred in the camps.[32]

When President Huerta resigned in August 1914, the United States made plans to release its Mexican army prisoners in September. The major problem was where to release them. Potential American employers said that if the soldiers were released in the United States they could provide them with jobs in the mines and railroads. Captain Estes had to deny requests from potential employers "ranging from day laborers to clear land, or pick cotton, through domestic servants of all classes, to children for adoption into American families."[33]

Since the United States had begun to favor Venustiano Carranza over Villa, the former *federales* of Huerta were put on trains and transported to Piedras Negras, Coahuila. The *federales* officers were not sent back to Mexico, but were allowed to stay in the United States. Usually, they were killed by the rebels, and sending them back to Mexico might have resulted in their immediate deaths. Train tickets to various parts of Texas, New Mexico, Arizona, and California were given to 275 officers, 125 *soldaderas*, and 80 children. Those *soldaderas* who went with the soldiers to Piedras Negras faced more army life, as most of the soldiers were incorporated into the army of Gen. Antonio Villareal, a follower of Carranza.[34] On January 8, 1915, these former *federales* troops "broke under the massive cavalry charge" of Gen. Emilio Madero at Ramos Arizpe in Coahuila. Some of them probably fled with other Carrancistas, while others became part of the three thousand prisoners of Madero and Felipe Angeles. In a gesture of kindness, the prisoners were freed if they swore not to rejoin the Carrancistas. What happened to the *soldaderas* in this series of battles is unknown.[35] In a last bit of irony, Mexico received from the United States a claim for $740,653.13, the cost of interning the federal soldiers and their families (*El Paso Morning Times* [September 11, 1914]).

The battles waged by Mercado and Villa against each other and the subsequent detainment of the *federales* in the United States show that *soldaderas* were integral components in these series of events. They fulfilled many roles in federal and rebel armies, which disputes the contention that women were not actively involved in most aspects of warfare. Just as Mexican attempts to eliminate the *soldaderas* from the ranks were largely unsuccessful, so too were American attempts to separate the *soldaderas* from the *soldados*.

We, the Women 5

It was there that I first saw Elizabetta. She was a very dark-skinned Indian girl, about twenty-five years old trudging . . . stolidly along the dust behind Captain Felix Romero's horse. . . . I found out later that . . . he had found her wandering aimlessly . . . apparently out of her mind, and that needing a woman, he had ordered her to follow him. Which she did, unquestioningly, after the custom of her sex and country.

—*John Reed*

Like many others, Reed described the *soldaderas* as self-sacrificing, silent, and obedient camp followers leading miserable lives before, during, and after the Revolution. But, as evidence indicates, these women did not always act as stoical and uncomplaining servants. An examination of nine life histories illuminates the diverse experiences and attitudes of the *soldaderas*. Scholars, activists, and a novelist all had occasion to record the life stories of women who fought as soldiers or followed troops during the Revolution. Their collective work dispels or qualifies the stereotypes found in Reed's conversation with "Elizabetta" and the ethnological re-creation of the *soldaderas* as promiscuous women in Ricardo Pozas's *Juan the Chamula*.

Oscar Lewis conducted an extensive study of the Sánchez family living in Mexico City. In *A Death in the Sanchez Family*, he includes the life history of an aunt, Guadalupe Vélez. She had been a *soldadera* during the Revolution and played a central nurturing role for the Sánchez children. Jane Holden Kelley for her study *Yaqui Women: Contemporary Life-Histories* interviewed two women, Chepa Moreno and Dominga Ramírez. Kelley's study is significant in that these two Indian women reacted positively to most of their experiences as *soldaderas*.

The abbreviated life history interview of María de la Luz Espinosa Barrera, which appears in Anna Macías's study *Against All Odds: The Feminist Movement in Mexico to 1940*, reveals the fiercely independent nature of "La Coronela" before and after the Revolution. Marta Romo's article "Y las soldaderas? Tomasa García toma la palabra" brings to light another individualist who struggled to survive the slums of Mexico City and who fought in vain to gain veteran's benefits.

Activists in the Chicano movement Esther R. Pérez, James Kallas, and Nina Kallas published a number of interviews with Mexican veterans who had emigrated to California (*Those Years of the Revolution, 1910–1920, Authentic Bilingual Life Experiences as Told by Veterans of the War*). The study includes a lengthy interview with Lt. Col. Angela "Angel" Jiménez and a brief account of María Villasana López's experiences as a *soldadera*. These life histories provide valuable information about army women who joined the large migration of Mexicans into the United States during and after the Revolution.

Film star Anthony Quinn in his autobiography, *The Original Sin*, includes a biographical sketch of his mother Manuela Oaxaca Quinn, who served as a *soldadera* for a short period. Quinn had much to say about her romantic illusions about men, the goals of the Revolution, and the hard realities of war. Mexican novelist Elena Poniatowska wrote a "docu-novel," *Hasta no verte Jesús Mío*, about *soldadera* Jesusa Palancares. She portrays Palancares as a woman who developed a strong independent identity and who loved different kinds of adventures.

I shall contrast life histories of these nine women with two well-known characterizations of the *soldaderas* by Reed and Pozas. Both men highlight the *soldaderas'* sexual relationships with soldiers. Reed, for example, was once "the other man." Elizabetta begged him to claim her for the night. Claiming fatigue, she did not want to commence sexual relations with her new soldier consort, Captain Romero.

> "My lover was killed yesterday in the battle. This man [Captain Romero] is my man, but, by God and all the Saints, I can't sleep with him this night. Let me stay with you!" There wasn't a trace of coquetry in her voice. . . . I doubt if she even knew herself why the thought of this new man so revolted her, with her lover scarcely cold in the ground. I was nothing to her, nor she to me. That was all that mattered. I assented, and together we left the fire.[1]

Reed has often been accused of creating fanciful stories of this kind to show his attractiveness to women. It is possible that a *soldadera* could have selected him to be her next "soldier-employer," but she probably would not have left Reed for another man (Reed had more money) just because a soldier "ordered" her to do so. If a soldier or officer wanted a woman to be his *soldadera* he had to show her either money or valuables, or perhaps try to woo her. Even if he took her by force, if she had strength of character, in time, she could leave him for another soldier-employer who caught her fancy or had more money.

Pozas also emphasizes sexual relationships between *soldaderas* and his main character, Juan Pérez Jolote. Pérez Jolote had his first sexual experiences with an "old woman with white hair" who sold *pulque* to the soldiers. In another encounter, while guarding pack animals, Pérez Jolote was accosted:

> One of the women that belonged to the soldiers came over and said, "Listen, José [Juan], let's go bathing in the river." She was really young, not like the woman who sold pulque, so I went with her. "Take off your clothes," she said. She was already undressed. We waded out into the river and she began to play by splashing water at me. After the third time I splashed back. She kept on splashing me, so I went over and embraced her, and that was when I knew what she was like and what she wanted.[2]

The *soldadera* then told Juan she was available any time he wanted her.

The view of the *soldaderas*, primarily as sexual beings, found in these popular and widely read books has marred an objective study of them. The *soldaderas* cannot be categorized into a single mold or type. They were as diverse as their experiences. They had differing family backgrounds, regional and class affiliation, and personalities. Personal histories provide insight into the complexity of the *soldadera* experience. In contrast to the unknown origins of the *soldaderas* drawn by Reed and Pozas, the nine women we shall study here who became *soldaderas* represented most regions of Mexico.

Born around 1896 in Jalapa del Márquez, Oaxaca, Angela Jiménez was the daughter of a Zapotec mother and a Spanish father, a political chief of Tehuantepec. She described him as a "rigid Spaniard," while she said her mother was always willing to give money, food, or compassion to the poor.[3] Jiménez did not like school, but instead enjoyed the freedom of the country and would spend her time there rather than in a classroom.

Jesusa Palancares was born about 1900 in Tehuantepec, but her family later moved to Oaxaca. Her mother died and she was left with only her father, a brother, and a series of stepmothers she despised. Palancares described her father as a wanderer, and Palancares herself lived with different families and performed domestic work.[4]

María de la Luz Espinosa Barrera was born about 1887 in Yautepec, Morelos. Her mother died at her birth and her father never remarried. She recalled a very lonesome childhood. When asked by other children where her mother was, she "pointed to a favorite goat amid the peals of laughter of her insensitive peers."[5] As a young woman, she spent five years in jail for killing her husband's mistress.

Guadalupe Vélez and Tomasa García Magallanes hailed from Central Mexico. Vélez was born in León, Guanajuato, in 1900, one of eighteen children, of whom only seven survived their first year. Her parents made sweets and sold them in the town plaza. From the age of five, Vélez took care of her younger siblings and did the marketing and the cooking. Her parents never allowed her to go to school and beat her if she wanted to play with other children.[6] This pattern coincides with the findings of Vivian M. Vallens in her study of working women during the Porfiriato. According to Vallens, "families remained rather loosely knit and children usually became independent and began to work at an early age."[7]

Born in 1902 at Labatos Valparaíso, Zacatecas, García Magallanes grew up on an hacienda and asserted her independent nature at a very early age. She hated school because the teacher would beat children who were slow learners.[8]

Four women were natives of the far northern states of Mexico. Manuela Oaxaca Quinn, born in Chihuahua City, Chihuahua, around 1898, described her ancestry as Indian. Her mother bore her out of wedlock and both mother and daughter washed and ironed clothes to survive.[9] María Villasana López, born in Chihuahua in 1902, resided in a small village with her mother and sister.[10]

An Indian born at La Colorada mine in Sonora around 1898, Dominga Ramírez, like most women of her region, spoke only Yaqui. Periodically, government troops would round up Yaqui men and women, as powerful Mexican landowners wanted their tribal lands. Deported from Sonora in 1904, Ramírez and her family were placed into debt peonage by the owner of the Hacienda Tanihl in the state of Yucatán.[11]

Chepa Moreno, also a native of La Colorada mine in Sonora, was born in 1899. She lived a good life until forced to marry at the age of fourteen. Then Mexican troopers captured her husband and slated him for deportation to the Yucatán. He informed the authorities of his marital status, which caused Moreno to resent him, because most Yaqui married men did not tell the authorities that they were married lest their wives and children share their fate. Moreno and her baby daughter were also deported to the Yucatán and sold as slaves.[12]

Some women lived in rural villages and haciendas but other women, like Vélez and Quinn, hailed from well-populated towns. They can be classified as working-class women. The three women from southern Mexico at an early age displayed adventuresome, aggressive, and restless behavior. García Magallanes, of Central Mexico, also shared these traits. Vélez, Quinn, Villasana López, Ramírez, and Moreno conformed to traditional expectations for Mexican women. Bitter family and conjugal relationships characterized the early life of all the *soldaderas* in my sample.

All nine women were eventually caught up in the vortex of war and factionalism that commenced in 1910. The women who served during the Revolution were both young and middle-aged. Some volunteered to fight while others followed their husbands or were abducted. *Soldaderas* participated in most phases of an army's day-to-day operations in the field. Far from being promiscuous or submissive, the *soldaderas* often expressed fierce independence and deep resolve in their relations with men. A degree of sisterhood emerged from the common struggles women faced during the war.

Women became *soldaderas* for a variety of reasons. María Antonieta Rascón argues that the *soldaderas*, as wives of soldiers, followed them without question. She doubts that the *soldaderas* had the intelligence to understand the goals of the Revolution.[13] Some of the nine women in my sample, however, seem well aware of the goals and ideals of revolutionary struggle.

Jiménez turned fifteen in 1911, the year *federales* searched her father's home for rebels. An officer tried to rape her sister but she grabbed the officer's gun and shot him before she killed herself. With this incident vividly imprinted in her mind, Jiménez joined her father in the Sierra Madre, vowing to become a soldier who killed *federales*. Jiménez disguised herself as a man and started calling herself "Angel," a name she preferred to use thereafter. One of her commanders engaged in political consciousness-raising. As she remembered, "he pointed out that the Revolution for me was an ideal which symbolized my dreams of pure justice. He knew that I was stubborn, and had a will to win, just like the Revolution itself."[14] Jiménez recalled memorizing the military codes of behavior as outlined in the Plan of San Luis Potosí endorsed by Francisco Madero.

When she was only fourteen, Palancares's soldier father decided to take her along. As his only living child, he wanted her always by his side. In 1910 Espinosa Barrera, at the age of twenty-four and standing no more than 4′8″, had just completed her jail sentence. She had returned to the state of Morelos to join her father in the Zapatista ranks.[15] García Magallanes, as an eight-year-old, joined her widowed mother and brothers in following Villa. Her family was persuaded by the oratory of Villa—"he who wants to be free . . . raise his hand and join my army." García Magallanes remembered raising her hand along with many others. She also felt sympathy because she believed that Villa fought to avenge the honor of his sister, who had been raped by a rich man.[16]

Two *soldaderas* followed soldiers because they had been raped or abducted. A thirty-two-year-old man raped Vélez at the age of thirteen. Her father forced her to marry him. Her husband then joined the Villistas and insisted that she accompany him.[17] Villista general Bonilla abducted fourteen-year-old Villasana López and her sister in 1916. She remembered that her mother "wept and pleaded for them to leave us with her, but not our tears, our panic, or our screams helped us at all."[18] Bonilla and his soldiers then fled to the Sierra Madre with the two girls.

In contrast, Quinn voluntarily followed her boyfriend. She was fifteen when he joined Villa's forces. He asked her if she would join him at the train station and become his *soldadera*. In love with the boy, Quinn decided to join him on the troop train. News about Villa's victories over the federal army convinced many people in Chihuahua that there could be change. As she remembered, "Maybe it wasn't God's law that some people should starve while others had plenty. Maybe the man who plants the lettuce can also eat the salad."[19]

In the early days of the Revolution, Villa attracted many women to his cause because they too believed that there might be changes made for the betterment of their lives. To many *soldaderas*, soldiering or following troops meant that they be allowed to do whatever they could to win the battles. As their battle experience grew, many women wanted to be recognized as heroic and powerful in their own right. In the camps, change meant that they could start or end relationships with men based on their needs. But their individual ideas of change often had to be disguised in patriotic rhetoric about the needs of male soldiers to fight well and for the country to do more for all of its citizens.

The two Yaqui women deported to the Yucatán had only one route out: to follow the troops. As a twelve-year-old, Ramírez and her mother followed the soldiers headed for Mexico City. When her mother married a well-paid Carrancista officer, Ramírez's life changed for the better.[20] The family traveled all over Mexico with him. In fact, Ramírez described herself as a pampered "army brat" who eventually married a soldier. At twenty-five, Moreno was abandoned by her husband in the Yucatán. She then followed the Yaqui troops to Mexico City. Moreno found that she could make more money by cooking for soldiers than by begging on the streets or washing dishes for street vendors. She met and married a Mayo Indian fighting under Carrancista general Chito Cruz. She boasted that she was a good cook. Moreno recalled with horror the battle of Celaya in April 1915, when the lines shifted directly into the women's camp, causing many casualties. After 1915, when Carranza's army moved into the state of Guerrero to fight Zapata, the *soldaderas* found the climate and environment unbearable. On one occasion, the soldiers abandoned them to chase after Zapata's troops, an incident that Moreno recalled as a "terrible, fearful time."[21]

Just as the nine women entered the Revolution in differing ways, so too did they participate in varying kinds of soldierly activities. Macías makes a distinction between those whom she calls women soldiers and the *soldaderas*. Female soldiers took on "male qualities" such as decisiveness, domination, and courage, while *soldaderas*, as true camp followers, stayed behind the lines, cooking and caring for their husbands or lovers.[22]

A survey of the nine women suggests that the differences between female soldiers and camp followers are less than clear-cut. Because of the changing configurations of battle lines, many times camp followers by necessity had to perform as soldiers with all the skill, resourcefulness, and aggression that survival required. On the other hand, female soldiers sometimes took a decidedly motherly attitude toward the welfare of their fellow male soldiers.

Jiménez served as a soldier, flag bearer, explosives expert, spy, and on occasion she made sure her fellow soldiers did not go hungry. As she remembered:

> I called about ten men together and we went in search of food. We found a hacienda that supposedly belonged to a North Ameri-

can Gringo and we broke the locks and headed directly for the
kitchen. . . . I ordered two men to kill the cow which was in the
corral and proceeded to take over the food operation. . . . Well, I
felt personally responsible for the ten men, but I did have my justi-
fications. I could not ignore that since I was the only woman
around I felt it was my obligation to feed the men who had been
near starvation.[23]

Jiménez recalled that she was happy that the men had food to last
a few days.

She referred to herself as "a volunteer who actively participated
but was never given promotions." Jiménez decided to approach
her commander and ask that she be officially counted as a soldier.
"My decision to speak up was much to my advantage. I was now
recognized as a soldier and taking care of myself was easier. I had
minor problems disguising myself, but the General of my troop
knew who I was and was obligated to keep an eye out for me."[24]
Jiménez quickly rose to the rank of lieutenant.

Even though disguised as a man, Jiménez always carried wom-
en's clothing with her. On one occasion, she had use for her change
of clothes. Her troop was captured and incarcerated; dressed as a
woman, she escaped. Then she convinced some *soldaderas* to help
her gather weapons and place them in a corn field. She planned to
help her fellow soldiers escape from jail, get the weapons, and
return to their army. Her plan was a success. Later in 1916, Jiménez joined her father's troop. His battalion was captured and the
men set for execution. No one suspected that she was disguised as a
man, so once again Jiménez devised a plan to get out of jail. She
convinced a *soldadera* who sold food to the prisoners to smug-
gle women's clothes in to her. "She returned with a blouse, skirt
and rebozo into which I changed. I carried her basket and we
both walked out of prison."[25] Jiménez then escaped to Juárez and
walked across the border to El Paso. The soldiers, including her father, were executed.

Palancares grew up in a *federales* troop as her father's companion. Even though dressed as a boy, she generally stayed behind the
lines with the other *soldaderas*. But occasionally, and by necessity,
she and the *soldaderas* had to engage in more soldierly activities.
She accompanied the federal *soldaderas* when they "decided" to
wander into Emiliano Zapata's territory. Hoping to avoid a battle,
the *soldaderas* convinced Zapata that the approaching *federales*
were too strong. So Zapata and his men fled from the area. The *sol-*

daderas then returned to their camp and gave detailed information about Zapata's forces. The commander of the troop, discovering that Palancares was a woman, forced her at the age of fifteen to marry a seventeen-year-old captain. The troop was then ordered north and she dutifully followed her husband. After he died in battle, the soldiers under his command asked Palancares, as the captain's wife, to lead them back to safer territory. She left the army after this episode but returned as a *soldadera* to join the *federales* during the Cristero Revolt in 1926.[26]

Espinosa Barrera, whom Macías refers to as "a woman soldier, not a soldadera," was also skilled with horses. She fought in many battles and, according to Macías, "dressed like a man, and thought like a man."[27] Zapata gave her a battlefield commission as lieutenant colonel. On the other hand, García Magallanes, whom Macías might describe as a *soldadera*, still traveled with the followers of Villa wearing her bandoliers and carrying her carbine.

Vélez tended to stay behind the lines during the battles. After her first husband died in battle, she began a "free union" with another soldier. When he was transferred north to Matamoros, Tamaulipas, she went with him. Vélez worked in a tortilla mill and cooked for twenty-two soldiers in order to earn money to send to her mother in Mexico City. She washed and ironed clothes for Gen. Joaquín Amaro and Gen. Felipe Angeles. General Amaro liked her work and paid her quite well for taking care of his uniforms.[28]

Abandoned when she became pregnant, Vélez recalled how her life changed. "I'd go to the river with my big belly, carrying a load of laundry on my head and I washed for the soldiers all day, half submerged in the water. What a life I led. All I ate were tortillas made of white flour, fried onions, and a can of condensed milk." She stayed with the army, "cooking beans and making tortillas for the troops during the day and barricading her door every night to keep out the soldiers."[29]

Vélez is a good example of how women could stay with armies whether they were married, abandoned, widowed, or single. The major prohibition in remaining with an army as an "unattached" woman was the minimal pay for cooking and other services. As Vélez indicated, living as an unattached *soldadera* was extremely hard.

Disciplining the troops and *soldaderas* was a major headache for most commanders in the field. Just about anyone, ranging from grandparents, adults, teenagers, and young children, could be part of a band of irregulars or of a rebel group. Villa more than any

other commander tried to keep the *soldaderas* under strict super-
vision and away from the front. Quinn recalled the many restrictions placed on the *soldaderas* who followed Villa. She remembered the men sitting in groups singing *corridos*, but the women
had to spend their time cleaning guns or sewing. She said that
when an officer ordered the women to get off the train and feed the
men, "all the women made a dash for the fields" to gather firewood. The men were ordered to fight, and the women watched
them go. When the battle ended, the *soldaderas* were ordered to
pick up their belongings and cook for the men. Once the *soldaderas*
were washing clothes when the order came for all pregnant women
to return home. Quinn had to leave, as "men didn't fight as well
when they had to worry about their pregnant women." [30]

Villasana López remembered being "given a rifle just like all the
other Adelitas [*soldaderas*]" but she could never bring herself to
use it. Instead, she helped in washing the wounds of the soldiers
and in caring for the sick. Many times the *soldaderas* "were half
naked from making bandages with [their] clothes." [31] She was pregnant when her soldier-consort abductor died.

All of the nine women, whether they were soldiers or camp followers, did more than just cook and care for the soldiers. Jiménez,
Palancares, Espinosa Barrera, and García Magallanes saw their
share of combat. Women like Quinn, Ramírez, Moreno, Vélez, and
Villasana López tended to fulfill domestic duties for soldiers. Obviously, Villasana López was also at heart a pacifist. Often the
kinds of soldierly activities in which they engaged depended on the
personality and desires of the women; they do not fall into neat
categories of soldier or camp follower.

The way the women related to soldiers and to other *soldaderas*
depended on their personality and sense of identity. *Soldaderas*
cited many instances when men sought to restrict their movements and forced them to submit. These women often complained
about male domination and sometimes resisted resolutely and
forcefully. Constantly frustrated by her superiors' failure to recognize her achievements, Jiménez verbally challenged General
Amaro, the future war minister, who barred the *soldaderas* from
the army in 1925. When the general expressed reservations about
women's role as soldiers, Jiménez responded that she did not
require the "vital organs of a man" to be a strong and courageous
soldier. Jiménez not only chided the general for his prejudice
against female soldiers, she also warned her fellow troopers about

amorous advances toward her. She said that she would "in no way hesitate in blowing out their brains."[32] She never had to back up her words with deeds.

Jiménez generally had positive things to say about the other *soldaderas* even though she considered them different from herself:

> I know of several women that joined the troops, not as "Adelitas" but as true soldiers. In Alaquines, Guadalupe Becerra joined our platoon. . . . In the one battle of Ebano, General Cedillo and Guadalupe Becerra were both killed. The women sometimes did not last long, but their courage and presence said a lot for the women of that time. Many of the soldiers' women would risk their lives to bring their men a cup of hot coffee during a battle. If the man happened to be killed, the woman would pick up his rifle and shoot along with the rest of us. I was lucky to make friends with them because they somehow always remembered to bring me something special.[33]

In this passage Jiménez distinguishes between soldiers and camp followers, but it has to be emphasized that on the battlefield even the "Adelitas" acted like soldiers.

Palancares described herself as very wild, dressing like a man because she "wanted to do men's things, to get into fights, to go to cockfights, to sing, and play the guitar when time permitted."[34] Once married, Palancares's husband locked her up in a room and said that she would remain there until she became more submissive. Her married life was filled with beatings and his affairs with other *soldaderas*. Palancares did not mind these affairs because she did not love her husband. She hit these women because they "made fun of her."[35] Finally, she took out two guns and told him to pick one up. If he beat her again, he would also have to kill her, because otherwise she would kill him. Her husband did not beat her again.

Palancares told stories about *soldaderas* who helped her and *soldaderas* who mistreated her. She distinguished between *soldaderas* who were the wives and daughters of soldiers and *soldaderas* who were not, whom she called whores and bitches. Palancares beat up her father's camp followers. She resented these women because they took her father's money to squander on liquor. One of her father's women, "La Guayabita," mistreated her, even calling her a whore. The other *soldaderas* in the camp were very much disturbed by this abuse. A large group of them told the general in charge about the abuse and demanded that he stop it. He immediately castigated her father for allowing such mistreatment.

Other *soldaderas* like Espinosa Barrera, Vélez, and García Magallanes were also disillusioned by marriage. Like Palancares, Espinosa Barrera was a woman who "smoked, drank, gambled and feared no man."[36] Because of the failure of her first marriage and subsequent incarceration, she was understandably very cautious in matters of the heart. Beaten by her first husband, she vowed to the Virgin of Guadalupe that she would never remarry (in a church or civil ceremony) because she had suffered so much as a wife. Vélez took her second soldier consort away from another *soldadera*, but refused to marry him. He was very jealous and quite restrictive. "He didn't allow me to raise my eyes or leave the door open, but he chased after other women all the time."[37] When Vélez became pregnant, her lover abandoned her.

García Magallanes was not married while she served in the army. She did have a couple of "free unions," which resulted in children. She did not give details about her love affairs; she only said she preferred to live alone.

Both Quinn and Villasana López loved their men, despite their shortcomings. Quinn had always had a desire for a husband who would be romantic, kind, and considerate. Her participation as a *soldadera* changed her ideas about romantic love and real love.

> Those first few battles had changed all my girlish ideas of love. We were not characters in a fairy tale. I wasn't waiting for my knight to come on a white charger. I was constantly afraid that the next charger would be black and that he would take my man. Love was ugly hours of waiting and fears. Love was cooking for your man as he went off to battle, mending his clothes when he returned. Love was giving thanks to God that your man was still alive.[38]

Quinn's relationship with her soldier consort did last. However, he was rarely romantic or considerate.

Abducted by General Bonilla, Villasana López in time came to like and respect him. But soon after she became pregnant, he died in battle. She and her baby daughter suffered from hunger, cold, and inadequate clothing in the snows of the Sierra Madre.

Ramírez and Moreno had relatively good experiences as *soldaderas*. Ramírez's mother fought another *soldadera* to "claim" an officer. The *soldadera* of an officer had more status and money than the *soldadera* of a low-paid enlisted man. Single, abandoned, or widowed *soldaderas* were the worst off because wages paid to them for labor in the camps were very small. The relationship between the soldier and the *soldadera* mirrors that of the officer-soldier and patron-peon hierarchies. Paul J. Vanderwood notes that in the officer-recruit relationship the federal soldiers' loyalty was to the superior officer, "who promoted and punished them and who might even have recruited them."[39]

As the adopted daughter of the officer and later as the wife of a soldier, Ramírez never had to wash clothes or grind corn for tortillas. She had good living quarters, nice clothes, and developed her talents for "dancing, talking brightly and looking decorative."[40] When her stepfather resigned from the army, he received a small pension. For Ramírez, the good times were over. She no longer had the money to buy many things. When her soldier husband left the army they returned to Sonora. Ramírez recalled that once her husband left the army and had little money, he became a different man and took to drinking too much. Moreno's second husband abandoned her for another woman after he was released from the army. Moreno requested train passage home from the Obregón government and returned alone to Hermosillo, Sonora. (She bore seven children but they all died at birth.) In Hermosillo she lived with a distant relative.[41]

The relationship of the *soldaderas* and the soldiers was often filled with frustration and abuse. Some women refused to marry, but rather preferred the liberty of "free unions." Women in the camps did at times fight with each other for men, especially for the more well paid officers. But, in general *soldaderas* admired and respected the valiant actions of their peers on the battlefields and in the camps.

After the Revolution, most of the nine women in my sample did not return to their towns or regions of origin. Some assessed the Revolution as a failure in many respects. For a few, especially those who migrated to the United States, their lives improved somewhat. While many returned to traditional styles of womanhood, others became pillars of strength in their local communities.

Three women did return to their hometowns. Espinosa Barrera remained in Morelos, a clothing vendor who traveled extensively. She qualified for a small pension as a veteran and lived until 1977. Her life remained to the end filled with the fierce desire for independence and freedom of action.[42] Ramírez and Moreno both returned to Sonora and lived in traditional Yaqui society until their deaths. Ramírez called her life as an officer's daughter and soldier's wife "rather privileged." She contrasted her life back in Sonora as "lacking freedom of movement" under the stern authority of her mother-in-law.[43] Moreno lived until 1970. For Moreno, her life as a *soldadera* was "a tremendous improvement over the years with Pedro in the Yucatan . . . during her soldadera years, it seems, Moreno enjoyed a role in which her being a Yaqui was not the key factor in other peoples' reactions to her."[44] Moreno's most vivid memories were of the Revolution and her experiences as a *soldadera*.

Three of the *soldaderas* moved to the slums of Mexico City. Palancares continued a life of adventure and hard living and delved into mysticism until she died in 1988.[45] García Magallanes worked at odd jobs and often had to rely on charitable establishments for shelter. She asked for a veteran's pension based on her military activities, but she was laughed out of the veterans' office.[46] García Magallanes, like Palancares, thought that Mexican society had betrayed those who fought in the Revolution. "We, who were the ones who fought the revolution, who suffered and bled, so that all could live in peace, were given the back of the hand."[47] Vélez died on November 2, 1962. In describing her death, Oscar Lewis wrote, "Guadalupe died as she had lived without medical care, in unrelieved pain, in hunger worrying about how to pay the rent or raise money for the bus fare for a trip to the hospital, working up to the last day of her life."[48] Vélez, like many *soldaderas*, was not eligible for veterans' benefits or hospital care afforded to some former soldiers.

Quinn, Villasana López, and Jiménez all left the army and even Mexico before the violent phase of the Revolution ended. They joined the large numbers of Mexican refugees who emigrated to the United States and later moved to California. Villasana López "worked very hard" in the United States "to make a living and to educate her daughter."[49] She was proud that her daughter headed a migrant farmworker program in Gilroy, California.

Quinn worked to support her son, actor Anthony Quinn, until she was reconciled with her husband. She contrasted the meaning of the Revolution for her and her soldier husband: "He romanticized the revolution. He thought the revolution would make it paradise on earth. To me it was just the smell of gunpowder and the crying of the wounded. I saw no romance in it. We were just poor people fighting for our stomachs, the talk of brotherhood and the flag waving came later from our suffering."[50]

Jiménez remained an outspoken woman and activist for a variety of causes. She helped to start the veterans' group La Organización de Veteranos de la Revolución de 1910–1920 in California. She persuaded Villasana López to tell her story for the benefit of young people who needed to understand the true story of the Revolution. Jiménez spoke many times before the San Jose City Council in Spanish about various issues of concern to Chicanos such as bilingual and bicultural education in the schools.[51] She tried to have children, but a doctor informed her that the tequila and gunpowder chaser many soldiers swallowed before battles to instill courage probably had made her sterile. Nonetheless, she adopted and cared for many children. Upon her marriage to Ramón Vásquez she made certain demands: "I would marry him if he accepted me as his equal and not as his weak wife who he could boss around. My children needed warmth and affection and if he was to accept me he must also accept all of my children. This was not an easy situation for a man to accept, but Ramón agreed and we were married."[52] Jiménez counted among her children many orphans, foster children, mentally and physically disabled. Part of Jiménez's philosophy related to her Zapotec Indian heritage. "We challenge life itself and many of us live to be in the hundreds. Each day is the beginning of a new life with new ways to attain a more harmonious existence with others."[53] She also believed that the strong should take care of the weak.

This chapter casts doubt on the stereotype of the *soldaderas* as women living miserable lives with little knowledge of themselves or the world around them. Like male soldiers who lived through the Revolution, the *soldaderas* had diverse reactions to the chaotic events that shaped their lives. The nine women profiled exemplify differences in relation to their early life, their experiences with armies, the goals of the Revolution, soldiers, other *soldaderas*, and their lives after the civil war. These women learned from their life experiences, demonstrated leadership, and maintained a confidence in their ability to survive and grow.

A woman warrior with a shield from the Remojadas culture, ca. A.D. 600–800. (*Natural History* 63, no. 5, May 1954)

Warrior Princess Six Monkey captures a prisoner. (Selden Codex, ca. A.D. 1035)

Doña Marina carrying a warrior's shield; she stands near a shrine to the goddess Toci. (Lienzo de Tlaxcala, plate 45, in Alfredo Chavero, *Antigüedades mexicanas*, 1892)

Coyolxauhqui defeated by her brother Huitzilopochtli, ca. A.D. 1143. (Museo Nacional de Antropología, Mexico City)

Uniforms worn by the Mexican army in 1845. (El soldado mexicano, 1837–1847, organización, vestuario, equipo y reglamentos militares. Mexico City: Ediciones Nieto, Brown, Hefter, 1958)

XVI a) Soldado, 4-o Baón., Inf. Ligera — Private, 4th Light Inf. Baon. 1846. b) Capellán Castreuse — Field Chaplain. c) Director de Hospital, Cuerpo Médico, Gala — Hospital Director, Medical Corp, Gala, 1846. d) Ayndte. J-o, Cuerpo Médico, Campaña — Adjt., Medical Corp, Field Dress, 1846. e) Enfermero de Ambulancia, Campaña — Ambulance Attendant, Field Dress, 1846. f) Soldadera — Soldier-Woman. g) Soldado, 1-er Regto., Caball. Permte., Nuevo Uniforme — Trooper, 1st Regular Caval. Regt., New Uniform, 1845.

Federal *soldados* and *soldaderas* resting after a battle. (Fondo Casasola, Fototeca del Instituto Nacional de Antropología e Historia, Pachuca Hidalgo)

Afro-Mexican woman revolutionary from Michoacán. (Fondo Casasola, Fototeca del Instituto Nacional de Antropología e Historia, Pachuca Hidalgo)

Soldaderas under the command of Adolfo de la Huerta, 1925. (Fondo Casasola, Fototeca del Instituto Nacional de Antropología e Historia, Pachuca Hidalgo)

Coronela Juana Ramona Vda. de Flores; known as "La Güera," she had fought in fourteen battles by 1914. (Illustrated London News Picture Library)

"La Generala" Petra Herrera. (Adán Montecón Pérez, *Recuerdos de un villista: Mi campaña en la revolución.* Mexico City, 1967)

Troop train for Francisco Villa in 1914; estimated troops include 17,000 men, 4,000 women, and 4,000 children. (*Sunset Magazine*, 1914)

Two mounted Villista *soldaderas. (Sunset Magazine,* 1914)

Villista *soldaderas* doing the laundry. (*Sunset Magazine,* 1914)

The Greatest Picnic of Modern Times

This Texas picnic party costs Uncle Sam $2,500 a day. It is a tremendous social success — a seven months' riot of fun. And the funniest thing of all about it is that the host continues to labor under a delusion that his guests would like to depart!

Drawn by Ch. Gatchell

Editorial cartoon lampooning Fort Bliss camp. (*Collier's Magazine,* August 1, 1914)

Federal troops at Presidio, Texas, after retreating across the Rio Grande, January 12, 1914. (Library of Congress)

Soldaderas and their children at Fort Bliss camp. (Library of Congress)

Matilde Martínez, a *soldadera* cooking at Fort Bliss camp. (Library of Congress)

Lt. Col. Angela "Angel" Jiménez. (Esther R. Pérez, and James and Nina Kallas, *Those Years of the Revolution, 1910–1920: Authentic Bilingual Life Experiences as Told by Veterans of the war.* San Jose, Calif.: Aztlán Today, 1974)

Doña María Félix with Jorge Mistral in Juana Gallo. (Paco Ignacio Taibo I., *María Félix: 47 pasos por el cine.* Mexico City: Joaquín Mortiz Planeta, 1985)

Chicanas performing the dance "La Adelita," in Seattle, Washington, September, 1982. (*La Voz*)

Chicana member of the Brown Berets in the 1960s; she wears bandoliers
as did the *soldaderas* of past wars. (Chicano Student Movement newspaper)

6 Adelita Defeats Juana Gallo

There were many types of soldaderas *in the Revolution: "La Valentina," modest and home-loving; "La Cucaracha," carefree, a woman for all, who gave her liquor and love with open hands; "Juana Gallo," the woman with fighting in her heart; but the most faithful and the most respected of the troop was "La Adelita," . . . the adorable sweetheart of the ranks.*

—Juan González A. Alpuche

On feast days in Mexica society, warriors danced with their constant companions, the *auianimes*. During the Revolution, soldiers sang about going to a dance at the camp with a *soldadera* named Adelita. After the Revolution, Mexicans continued singing about the *soldaderas*. Consequently, the *soldaderas* have become stock characters in literature, *corridos*, art, and films.

Works that contain *soldadera* characters tend to fall into two categories. Some have only one kind of *soldadera*, usually of the self-sacrificing, heroic camp follower type. The message behind this characterization is that women in armies and warfare were all self-abnegating types. Other works like the "Revolución" medley by Ballet Folklórico de México have many *soldadera* characters. These works are more reflective of the varied experiences of the *soldaderas*.

Yet even with this panoramic view, the "Adelita" *corrido* with its *soldadera* with a "heart of gold" and "sweetheart of the troops" dominates in Mexican culture. Sometimes when an artistic endeavor (mostly in films) is based on a *corrido* about a fearless, self-willed, outspoken female soldier (Juana Gallo), the storyline is compromised by adding a complicated love life. The theme usually centers around a domineering *soldadera* who has several romantic relationships and rivalries with other women to overcome. By film's end Juana Gallo has rechanneled her energies and become more like La Adelita in her self-abnegating, patriotic behavior.

Literature

Most scholars of the *soldaderas* (e.g., Mendieta Alatorre, Turner, Soto, Macías, and Leal) have discussed them as characters in literature and the arts. While all of these studies contribute to a better understanding of the *soldadera* in popular culture, none can be viewed as comprehensive, nor does any study consider the *soldadera's* literary ancestors. Both Indian and Spanish-language literature contain legends about Amazons and female camp followers, which became the basis for later characterizations of the *soldaderas*.

Among the early antecedents of *soldadera* stories are legends about warrior women in Indian societies. "The Warrior Princess" in the Selden Codex refers to a legend about a Toltec woman, "Six Monkey," who fought and defeated the men who insulted her. In Mexica society, the custom of the *auianimes* dancing with warriors in the barracks serves as the prototype of the most popular *corrido* of the Revolution, "La Adelita."

Spaniards like other Europeans had a fascination with Amazons. Finding Amazons was important to them because they allegedly occupied lands loaded with treasure. Because they were reputed to be fierce fighters, once subdued, they would make excellent allies. And by conquering an Amazon, a man proved he was a hero. Medieval tales about Amazons graced Spanish, Portuguese, Italian, French, German, and English literature.[1]

"La Doncella Guerrera" (the Maiden Warrior), a popular Spanish ballad, can be traced to the sixteenth century. The story concerns a count who had seven daughters and no son. The youngest daughter decided to dress like a boy and enlist in the army to fight in the wars between France and Spain. During her service, a prince suspected her true identity and fell in love with her. After she left the army, she returned to her father's home, put on a dress, and awaited her prince.[2] This ballad joins the historical reality of Spain's many wars with the social prescription that women should fulfill their ultimate destiny as wives and mothers.

Spaniards were particularly fascinated with Amazons found in the pages of *Amadis* (ca. 1492) and the *Esplandián* series (ca. 1510). García Rodríguez de Montalvo is considered either the author or translator of these sixteenth-century works. In *Esplandián*, Calafia, the queen of the Amazons, lives with her followers on the island California. Calafia joins forces with the king of Persia against

Christian knights Amadis and his son Esplandián. In battle, the Amazon women get the better of the Christians. The knights regroup and Calafia and her Amazons surrender. In submission the Amazons become Christians and allies of the knights. Although Calafia is in love with Esplandián, she agrees to obey his order and marry a knight selected for her.[3]

Spanish soldiers, including Hernán Cortés, took seriously the story of Calafia and her island with its wealth of gold and jewels. In fact, when Spanish soldier-explorer Juan Rodríguez Cabrillo in 1542 landed on new shores, he named the area California.[4]

A few *soldadera* characters are found in Mexican fiction from the sixteenth to the nineteenth centuries. While one portrayal relates the belligerent activities of a female soldier, other character sketches are thin and promote the miserable-camp-follower genre. The adventurous life of soldier Catalina de Erauzú (1592–1650) (profiled in chapter 2) was the subject of the first Mexican novel, *La monja alférez*.[5] A prototype of the miserable *soldadera* can be found in Luis G. Inclán's 1865 novel *Astucia*, wherein Inclán gives a unique description of rural life and the speech of the people and the character Elisa, a *soldadera*, descends to the lowest rung of society—a female servant to soldiers in the camps.[6] Angel de Campo emphasizes the filth of the *soldaderas* and calls them "dogs" of the troops in his 1894 short story "El fusilado." Esteban Maqueo Castellanos in his novel *La ruina de la casona* refers to the *soldaderas* as parasites who feed on armies.

Tomochic by Heriberto Frías appeared in the periodical *El Demócrata* in 1892. *Tomochic* is considered both a novel and a fairly accurate account of an army campaign against villagers in Chihuahua. One of its themes is the vision of the *soldaderas* as redemptive entities. Frías was very disillusioned by Porfirian society's brutal division of the rich and poor, the greed of the elite class, and the ruthlessness of the army. He was awed by the loving care the *soldaderas* gave the soldiers despite their own misery and poverty. Because the *soldaderas* did all they could for the men, they served as a redemptive force. Their actions harked back to earlier, more primitive, times when a child always returned to the mother for comfort and security. Yet for Frías, the downside was that they were not from the elite class. Rather, the *soldaderas*, as Indian women, were from the less-esteemed (and therefore less-acceptable) element in Mexican society.[7] Later novelists would promote the redemptive and maternal qualities of the *soldaderas* and, just like

Frías, condemn coarseness or lack of femininity in their *soldadera* re-creations.

Depictions of *soldaderas* during the Revolution tended to be part eyewitness account and part fiction. Authors would describe the soldierly activities of the *soldaderas* but at the same time portray them as good, feminine, pathetic camp followers or bad, ruthless female soldiers who seemed out of control. Sometimes literature about the *soldaderas* hinged on shallow notions of good and bad women.

Both an Amazon and a camp follower emerge as characters in the most well known and popular novel of the Revolution. *Los de abajo* (The Underdogs) by Mariano Azuela appeared in newspaper installments in 1915. The novel relates the military adventures of Dr. Azuela with a rebel group affiliated with Pancho Villa. The protagonists are poor *campesinos* (farmers) turned outlaws.

La Pintada (the Painted One) and Camilla appear as the two main female characters. According to Luis Leal, La Pintada actually existed. She was the companion of Col. Maximiliano Hernández. Calling any woman in Mexico "La Pintada" is considered a form of disrespect. Azuela further shows his contempt for female soldiers by calling La Pintada a "vulgar wench, with rouged cheeks, dark brown arms and neck."[8]

La Pintada joined the troop of Demetrio Macías at the Battle of Tierra Blanca, Chihuahua, in 1913. Like other soldiers, she ransacks houses, takes clothing, jewelry, and horses. She wants to be the only woman with Macías's band, but gentle Camilla upstages her.

Macías falls in love with Camilla and takes her with him as his *soldadera*. While La Pintada prefers an abusive and excessive band of soldiers, Camilla urges Macías to discipline his troops. He even tells La Pintada, one of the troop's most ruthless soldiers, to leave the camp. Infuriated, La Pintada stabs and kills Camilla. In retaliation, Macías orders La Pintada to depart from the camp.

The depictions of La Pintada and Camilla often seem to hinge on extremes of good and bad. La Pintada, the Amazon, has few redeeming qualities, while Camilla, the maternal camp follower, seems the epitome of submissiveness and goodness.[9]

Azuela's 1918 novel *The Flies* portrays the *soldaderas* as primitive, base women. The story centers on the Reyes-Téllez family's trip on Villa's troop train. *Soldaderas* appear everywhere the family looks. Two *soldaderas*, described as the general's women, are rude and with their tasteless finery proclaim to everybody that they are crude country girls brought in by the soldiers from Durango or Chihuahua. Other *soldaderas* appear as "ragged, exhausted, sick-looking soldier women all skin and bones with angry and despairing faces."[10] Unfortunately, Azuela never goes beyond stark and negative descriptions of the *soldaderas*.

Unlike his description of the *soldaderas*, Azuela's description of the army riding the trains is realistic but grim: "Hammocks slung between truss rods, with fat women bouncing in them like fish caught in a net. Naked children, soldiers red-eyed and filthy. Withered faces gathered at the doors. Slowly, the cars rolled past. A little altar went by, decorated with wild roses and pictures of the Virgin. From a window hung a cage with a lark in it. In another a broken crock did duty as a flower pot."[11] The army train often served as part transport, part home for the soldiers and their families.

Rafael F. Muñoz wrote short stories for two anthologies, *Se llevaron el cañón para Bachimba* and *Si me han de matar mañana*. He characterizes *soldaderas* as camp followers integral to the functioning of the troops. Many of his stories emphasize their heroic and self-sacrificing feats. In "Villa ahumada" a *soldadera* dies after alerting soldiers about an ambush; in "Agua" a woman dies trying to get her soldier some water; and in "El niño" *soldaderas* bravely unload the ammunition from a fire-engulfed train.[12]

Nellie Campobello has the distinction of being the only well-known female author to write about her experiences during the Revolution. Her anthology *Cartucho* contains thirty-three portraits of revolutionaries. "La Nacha Ceniceros," a brief sketch of a Villista *coronela*, has two parts. First, Ceniceros accidentally kills her lover and Villa has her executed. Then the "real story" reveals that Ceniceros, "who tamed ponies and rode horses better than many men,"[13] fought to avenge her father's murder. Campobello says that she could have been a "famous *coronela*" but early on she tired of war and left to rebuild her home. Then Campobello inserts her political bias by saying that just as Ceniceros had exposed lies about her, so too would the lies against Villa be brought to light. In "Agustín García" Campobello praises her mother's bravery in saving a young girl from abduction.

By the 1940s, novelists had turned away from isolated episodic narratives to a larger, more unified view of the Revolution as a living entity. In his novel *Tropa vieja*, Francisco L. Urquizo, a former general, captures the different stages of the Revolution through the eyes of a soldier conscripted into various armies. His portrait of the *soldaderas*, however, basically presents a primeval world, where the *soldaderas* are always the same—humble, submissive women who feed and sleep with soldiers for pay.[14]

La negra Angustias by Francisco Rojas González presents a psychological study of a female revolutionary. The popular story won the highest honor for fiction, the Premio Nacional de Literatura, in 1944. A growing fear in Mexico at the time, expressed by psychologist Francisco González Pineda, suggested that the Revolution "broke up the family, increased the mother's power and influence over the children, while separating the father from his family."[15] The unnatural power of the female revolutionary became a major issue in Rojas's novel. The central figure, Angustias Farrera, is a mulatta whose mother died early and whose father went to prison. She had unpleasant sexual experiences as a child and the trauma of these events affected her sexual development.[16] She and her father join the Zapatistas in the state of Guerrero. As her father's daughter, Angustias automatically assumes command of his rebel band when he dies. She has a readiness to fight and a willingness to kill. Angustias puts on the uniform of a lieutenant, but she replaces the medal of Our Lord of Chalma on the cap with one of Our Lady of Guadalupe. She says she does "not need machos to defend" or protect her.[17]

As "La Coronela" she disciplines her troops whenever they assault women or villagers. She castrates one man as an example. A powerful leader, La Coronela paradoxically falls in love with an effeminate and timid teacher. At the start of the relationship, the teacher thinks that women should not meddle in men's affairs by leading them into battle. La Coronela counters with the observation that "it is only because things have been left up to men that all things are unequal."[18] But La Coronela's true (feminine) nature emerges. She seduces the teacher, marries him, and has a child. Her husband then neglects her and has an affair with another woman.

La negra Angustias continues the tradition of an Amazon woman who tries to be a leader in a man's world. The author views Angustias's authoritative personality as a potentially deadly virus, which could lead to a nervous breakdown. The best cure for her sick personality is to love, marry, and serve a man. In submitting to the teacher, she discovers her true identity as wife and mother.[19]

As the Revolution became distant in people's memories, the image of the *soldaderas* became more romanticized and somewhat sedate. José Alvarado commented in the November 24, 1954, issue of *Siempre* that "Adelita was now Doña Adela" and she had become opulent, obese, and slightly diabetic.[20] Unlike Angustias, who asserts her dominance and superiority over men, the *soldadera* character starting in the 1950s possesses few flaws. The *soldadera* characters in Luis Zavalza Escandón's novel *Soldadera* tend to be feminine and ultranationalistic. As a career officer of thirty-two years, Zavalza Escandón viewed the *soldaderas* as good, selfless companions to the soldiers, "noble women and true mothers of the humble class."[21] His typical *soldadera* is a woman who goes with her soldier "out of love" and does not hesitate to give her life for him or for her country.

Carlos Isla in the 1980s wrote two short novels, *La Valentina* and *La Adelita*. These novels are easily found in paperback in both Mexico and the U.S. Southwest. Isla's *soldaderas* are extremely conscious of themselves as women seeking equality. The worldwide women's movement probably played a role in his emphasis. Gone are depictions of *soldaderas* as vulgar, crude, and ruthless. Instead, they have relations with soldiers who act as gentlemen and understand that women are men's equals in the fight for social justice.[22]

Soldaderas in *The Old Gringo* by Carlos Fuentes live for the happiness of the soldiers. They are first presented as just women of the troop. One woman, "La Garduña," became a *soldadera* because "a boy caught my eye, a boy who moved and seemed to call to me."[23] The "old gringo" character of the novel, Ambrose Bierce, also has an encounter with a *soldadera* who seems to remind him of primeval times. He "felt humiliated in the patient presence of the moon-faced woman in the blue rebozo. Her moist eyes revealed a deep, wise self-possession."[24] One *soldadera* suggests that an American character, Harriet, become a *soldadera* after she has sex with a Mexican general. "I follow my man, I cook for him and bear his children," she says, ". . . Will you be going with him? . . . Aren't you his new woman?"[25] Perhaps Fuentes believes that American women should be more like the *soldaderas* who represent love, sex, basic primitive reality, and submissiveness in much of Mexican literature.

Depiction of the *soldaderas* in literature since Mexica times has paralleled their presence in indigenous, Spanish, and Mexican armies. In many instances, novelists, as former soldiers, base their observations about *soldaderas* on their experiences in the field. A common theme is the way in which warrior women leave the fighting to men and resume their traditional roles as wives and mothers. The *soldadera* has emerged in Mexican literature as an ultranationalistic patriot who serves as a reminder to Mexicans that heroic abnegation on behalf of the homeland is important. But at the same time, constant recognition of the armed *soldadera-*patriot suggests undercurrents of potential change in attitudes toward women in a male-dominated society.

Corridos

The *corridos* of the Revolution represent even more than literature the heartbeat of the Mexican community. The *corrido's* origins come from the *romances* of fifteenth-century Spain, of which the *carrerilla* and the *jácara* (merry ballad) are variations. The *carrerilla,* or Andalusian *corrio,* came to Mexico with the conquistadors. From this evolved the *corrido.*[26] Like literature, *corridos* tell of various kinds of *soldaderas,* ranging from the female soldier to the camp follower. Most of the *corridos* about the *soldadera* are sung from the viewpoint of lovesick men. Unlike *corridos* about male revolutionaries like Villa and Zapata, none of the well-known *corridos* about *soldaderas* give their real names or are biographical. Consequently, there are very few stanzas that ring true about women in battle or in the camps.

The *corridos* reflect the different phases of the Revolution. "La cucaracha" (The Cockroach) is an old *corrido* that goes back to the nineteenth century. Fernán Caballero, a Spaniard, wrote one of the first stanzas of this satirical *corrido.* It became Mexican during the French Intervention when the French were made fools of by Porfirio Díaz. In time, Porfirian soldiers sang about "La cucaracha," a *soldadera* in the peacetime army who wanted money to go to the bullfights. With the Villistas, "La cucaracha" wanted money for alcohol and marijuana. She was often so drunk or stoned that she could not walk straight.[27]

Another early and exceptional *corrido* featured pleas from men for women to join them in war. A recruitment *corrido,* "La chinita maderista," asks a woman to join her male companion: "If you truly want me as I want you, we must go and fight for Madero."[28] The woman who accompanied her man might have gone out of love, but it should be remembered that her duties were to provide him with food and other personal necessities.

"La soldadera," a *corrido* of twenty-eight lines, deals with a soldier going to battle who hopes that his woman will join him: "Come with me, Juana, come with me . . . your eyes are the only bridge against the enemy who knows how to kill."[29] Robert Redfield notes in a song by a Zapatista soldier how important it was to get a *soldadera* to go along with you:

> Although they are enemies of our cause
> The Federal of my land have turned *guaches* (*soldaderas*),
> so they even sigh for a Federal trooper.
> As those fellows have plenty coin,
> So they get a good price for their love,
> So now they too say, "Down with Zapata."[30]

This story criticizes *soldaderas* who are not loyal to their men and seek out soldiers who have the most money.

As the level of violence increased, *corridos* appeared that portrayed aggressive women with guns or rifles. A *corrido* about a female officer, "La güera," depicts the leadership capabilities of women:

> The Blond One and her people
> dig their trenches.
> Although she is a woman who holds the rank of colonel
> her braids do not get in the way of her stars.[31]

"Juana Gallo" (the Rooster Woman) tells the story of a fearless woman in the midst of battle. The first stanza places her in the battlefield:

> Among the noise of cannons and shrapnel
> comes forth a popular story
> about a youth called Juana Gallo
> because she was valiant without a doubt.

The second stanza puts her in battle armed with a pistol.

> Always at the front of the troop you saw her
> fighting like all other soldiers
> in battle no federal soldier escaped her
> without mercy she shot them with her big pistol.[32]

The issue of whether Juana Gallo really existed became the subject of a book by Ignacio Flores Muro, *La verdadera Juana Gallo*.

Flores Muro claims that the real Juana Gallo, Angeles Ramos, lived in Zacatecas from 1876 to 1958. This woman did not fight or lead troops into battle as a colonel. According to Flores Muro, she spent most of her life in Zacatecas selling tacos and drinking tequila. He argues that the real Juana Gallo was not capable of thinking about the great and noble ideals of the Revolution. Flores Muro's efforts to downplay the Juana Gallo *corrido* appear consistent with the trend in literature to change the image of the warrior *soldadera* to a more pathetic image.[33]

In actuality, María Soledad Ruiz Pérez is the woman who was nicknamed Juana Gallo. In 1983 she was 103 years old and living in Ciudad Juárez. Her father and eight hundred other Villistas were murdered by General Carranza during the Revolution. She and four hundred women fought in one of the battles at Torreón. Her small government pension kept her in substandard housing with little furniture and even fewer belongings.[34]

A popular *corrido* about a *soldadera* armed with a pistol is "La rielera" (Railroad Woman). In one verse La Rielera sings "I have a pair of pistols / with ivory handles / to fight / those soldiers from the trains." "La rielera" had other verses, which depicted her as a camp follower who had an immense love for "Juan" the Mexican army's nickname for the common soldier.[35] "Marieta" is another *corrido* about a Villista female fighter, María del Carmen Rubio de la Llave. While the *corrido* is a traditional one, during the Revolution soldiers impressed by the allure of a particular woman would call her Marieta. Unfortunately, "Marieta" has no verses about brave or armed *soldaderas*. One verse tells of a soldier who "lost his head for a coquette, / a hussy named Marieta / who was the girlfriend of all the troop."[36]

"La Valentina" represents another *corrido* that predates the Revolution. Frías claims that the tune comes from Sinaloa. It became identified with Valentina Ramírez, a female soldier photographed by Agustín Casasola in 1913.[37] Not a single verse in this *corrido* mentions her actions on the battlefield. As a consequence, none of the words have been altered.

Such is not the case with the most well known *soldadera corrido*, "Adelita." The verses came from Villa's soldiers, but the melody may well have been a traditional favorite. There exist several versions. Adelita may have been the fourteen-year-old girl who nursed soldier Antonio del Río back to health. In another version, Adela was a twenty-one year old from Chihuahua who told Villa he should be the president of the Republic. Villa was attracted to her,

much to the dismay of her boyfriend, Pancho Portillo, who consequently committed suicide.[38] A few months later Villa asked his
guitarist to sing him a new song. The man sang "La Adelita,"
which he said was a story about Adelita and her dead boyfriend,
Portillo.

In another version of the story La Adelita is a woman who dis-
guises herself as a Dorado (golden one), a forbidden act, since Villa
barred women soldiers from the elite Dorados. But she dons the
distinctive clothes of the Dorados and falls in the first battle of
Celaya. Villa is angry because he did not want the Dorados to fight
in the early stages of the battle. When he discovers that Adelita is
the dead soldier, he pays her the highest compliment by saying
"She was a Dorado."[39] According to Tomasa García, a real *soldadera*, Adelita was a woman from Ciudad Juárez, Chihuahua. She
was said to have told the soldiers that if they were afraid, they
should stay in camp and cook beans. The real Adelita, according to
García, also told soldiers that she would wound or kill cowards.[40]

Nevertheless, the soldiers who sang about La Adelita did not
focus on her valor, but rather on her beauty, desirability, and loyalty. Only two lines from the first stanza point out that she was valiant and that the colonel respected her bravery. Then the *corrido*
boasts about how far a soldier would go for her love:

> If Adelita ever left with another
> I would follow her by land and by sea
> If by sea, in a powerful warship
> If on land on a military train.[41]

In another stanza the singer hoped that Adelita would always remember him:

> If I die in battle
> and my body will be
> buried in the Sierras
> Adelita, I implore you
> cry for me.[42]

Obviously, soldiers chose to sing verses that depicted Adelita as a
loyal camp follower with a heart of gold.

"Corrido del norte" by Pepe Guizar represents a Villista com-
pilation of the three *soldaderas* Adelita, Valentina, and Marieta.

The singer proudly asserts that he is a "pure Mexican" and not a Texan. He links his *norteño* identity with the *soldaderas* of his country. Adelita is a virtuous, pretty girl; Valentina is a colonel who still nurses his wounds; and Marieta is the girlfriend of all the troop.[43]

In "Yo me muero donde quiera" (I Die Anywhere), a woman sings about herself and other *soldaderas*. One line says that "women's shawls resembled bandoliers." Another verse claims that

> Women and men
> Give their lives for the country
> with valor
> Valentina, Jesusita already fought
> but they never die
> Adelita never dies
> always fighting by the side of her soldier.[44]

The diffusion of the *corridos* began during the Revolution with the military choirs, a standard feature of most Mexican regiments during the civil war. The choirs sang *corridos* and regional music. As these regiments traveled the country, the different *corridos* became widely disseminated. Choirs were also a regular feature of larger factories, and choral singing was taught in the schools.[45]

Manuel M. Ponce, a music teacher and composer, published early collections of "La Adelita" and "La Valentina" in 1913–1914, *corridos* "arranged in the romantic nineteenth-century salon style."[46] With the start of radio broadcasting in 1923, and the start of a record industry during the same decade, the *corridos* of the Revolution continued to be heard and recorded. Spinoffs of the *soldadera* theme can be found in such polkas as "Las coronelas" and "Las capitanas."[47]

Through the massive diffusion of the *corridos* and the popularity of the tune "La Adelita," the *soldaderas* became known as "Adelitas." "Las Adelitas," by Bonifacio Collazo (1961) concerns two Adelitas (*soldaderas*) who fight one another over a soldier.[48] The Ballet Folklórico de México labels its repertoire about the Revolution "Las Adelitas." Even Tomasa García, a real *soldadera*, acknowledged as much when she said, "To all we were Adelitas, because we were revolutionaries, we were of the army."[49]

"Dónde estás, Adelita," a 1980s version of the *corrido*, asks, "Where are you Adelita / where are you Warrior Woman?" Other stanzas honor the *soldaderas* as mothers:

> All of life is from your life
> all dreams come from your dreams . . .
> if it were not for you
> we would not be alive.[50]

The resurgence of the Adelita *corrido* in Mexico might be attributed in part to the visibility of Nicaraguan and Salvadoran guerrillas and female soldiers.

Musically, there is considerable linkage between Mexican and Nicaraguan music and culture. Sandino was influenced enough by the Mexican *corrido* "La Adelita" to make it his favorite camp song in the 1930s. So it is possible that for many Mexicans, lulled by the social re-creation of the *soldadera,* reporting on Nicaraguan female fighters may rekindle interest in women in the army. In fact, a Mexican woman, Aracelly Pérez, fought in Nicaragua and died in battle.

The most popular *corridos* of the Revolution focused on *soldaderas* as girlfriends and lovers. Lesser-known *corridos* that depict *soldaderas* as armed and dangerous represent an awareness that women since the Revolution have leadership ability and can be quite aggressive.

Art in the Modern Era

The nationalistic wave from the 1910 Revolution that imbued writers and ballad singers also had an impact on artists. As with other kinds of cultural expression, artists drew or painted *soldaderas* fulfilling different roles. Well-known female revolutionaries appear more often in engravings than they do in other works of art. Guadalupe Posada (1852–1913) boosted the art form by either creating or sponsoring about twenty thousand engravings listed under his name. Many of the engravings were made to enhance the texts of *corridos.* He drew *soldaderas* as "beautiful, well-groomed and determined young ladies."[51] Mostly the *soldaderas* wear dresses, sombreros, bandoliers, and carry rifles. A properly attired *soldadera* with rifle and bandolier appears on "The maderista," a collection of songs. Posada illustrated many pamphlets with *calaveras* (stylized skeletons). His "Calavera soldadera" shows a *soldadera* skeleton wearing a dress and armed with a pistol. She swings a lasso while riding a black horse over skeleton children.

This *soldadera* skeleton, sometimes referred to as a *"capitana"* or an "Adelita," might be considered a modern version of the ancient Mexica goddess Cihuacóatl, also depicted in skeleton form. The skeleton motif found in Mexican art symbolizes different ideas of equality. Skeletons do tend to look alike, thereby negating "all values, all differences, . . . the deceit that social conventions lend to them."[52]

Four great muralists, Diego Rivera (1886–1957), David Alfaro Siqueiros (1896–1974), Rufino Tamayo (1899–   ), and Jose Clemente Orozco (1883–1949), all portrayed *soldaderas* in their art. *Soldaderas* appear among the hundreds of persons in massive murals that depict the various groups who participated in the Revolution. Diego Rivera's *The Dream of a Sunday Afternoon in the Alameda*, in the Prado Hotel in Mexico City, depicts the history of Mexico. One recognizable *soldadera* appears in this mural of over one hundred people. She wears a sombrero and crossed bandoliers and carries a rifle and stands at the side of her male soldier companion, who rides a horse.[53]

David Alfaro Siqueiros's mural *Leaders of the Revolution* shows unarmed *soldaderas* standing by the side of male soldiers. These *soldaderas* wear rebozos and often appear to have a baby in their arms. Rufino Tamayo as a muralist followed a very personal direction. His works often depict a person's emotions. Tamayo's *Revolution*, a fragment, shows a *soldadera* wearing crossed bandoliers, in a tormented moment screaming out her anguish.[54]

José Clemente Orozco, judged by many to be the best Mexican muralist, created many etchings and pictures of *soldaderas*. Orozco depicts *soldaderas* as camp followers, armed women, or prostitutes. Shifra M. Goldman says that Orozco had "an antipathy" to the *soldaderas*. In *Soldier's Wife*, part of the fresco *Deserted Field*, and "The Mother's Farewell," *soldaderas* as devoted mothers and wives resignedly see their men off to war. In the lithograph *Soldaderas*, the oil paintings *On the March, Revolutionaries, Return to the Battlefield, In the Mountains*, and the illustrations for Mariano Azuela's *The Underdogs*, the *soldaderas* appear as obedient wives carrying babies and bundles while following the soldiers. The motif of women armed with rifles appears in his 1940 mural *Mother Mexico*. In this work a large eagle protects an Indian woman, who depicts the standard symbol of Mexico. In one of the wings of the eagle, three women wearing sleeveless dresses stand guard with rifles. Orozco also drew *soldaderas* as prostitutes. In one etching,

La cucaracha (1915–1917), half-dressed, drunken *soldaderas* wearing bandoliers and pistols stand by soldiers neatly dressed in their uniforms.[55]

Juan O'Gorman, another noted muralist, distorted female fighters by stressing their gender over their actions. In *History of the Tarascan Indians*, Érendira (from the Spanish Conquest) is barebreasted as she rides a white horse carrying a spear. In his mural *Francisco Madero*, housed in Chapultepec Castle in Mexico City, he depicts a mulatta *soldadera*. Agustín Casasola photographed this *soldadera* during the Revolution. The photograph shows the woman seated, armed with a pistol, and wearing pants. O'Gorman painted her standing, wearing a dress, and unarmed. Only men in his mural carry weapons. While O'Gorman depicted male soldiers realistically, he obviously distorted reality by painting female fighters not as they actually dressed but as he thought they should have appeared.[56] Roberto Montenegro in his oil painting *After the Battle* shows *soldaderas* searching for their wounded or dead soldier husbands. All the *soldaderas* are unarmed and carry babies.

Artists such as Jesús Escobedo, Fernando Castro Pacheco, Alfredo Zalce, Fernando Leal, Francisco Goitia, Manuel Rodríguez Lozano, and Alberto Beltrán also depict *soldaderas* in various realistic roles. Both Escobedo and Castro Pacheco deserve praise because in their engravings they portray well-known historical women, not just anonymous *soldaderas*. Escobedo sketched Doña Antonio Nava de Catalán (heroine of 1810 wars of independence) and Pacheco drew Carmen Serdán firing some of the first shots against Díaz forces on November 18, 1910. Zalce in the engraving *Soldadera* shows a woman binding the wounds of a fallen soldier. Leal in *Zapatista Camp*, shows a *soldadera* dressed in festive clothes serving food to the soldiers. In *Revolutionary Dance*, Goitia depicts vague, faceless *soldaderas* dancing with soldiers. In Rodríguez Lozano's *The Revolution*, six *soldaderas* mourn a fallen soldier. Beltrán made two paintings featuring *soldaderas*. His engraving *The Draft* depicts *soldaderas* being marched off by soldiers to cook and take care of them. In *Fighters against the Dictatorship*, two women wearing bandoliers and carrying rifles stand alongside the male soldiers while other *soldaderas* prepare food in the background.

Elena Huerta, Sarah Jiménez, Mariana Yampolsky, and Andrea Gómez also depict *soldaderas* in some of their works. Huerta in two engravings portrays Doña Josefa Ortiz de Domínguez (heroine of the wars of independence) and Leona Vicario (1813) holding a rifle. Jiménez sketched a dark-faced, shadowy engraving of Carmen Serdán armed with a rifle and wearing a bandolier. In her engraving *Revolutionaries' Bivouac* Yampolsky shows a campsite in which *soldaderas* are singing with the men while in the background others are making tortillas. The singing *soldadera* wears one bandolier and appears to be smiling. This happy woman is unique among portraits of *soldaderas*. In Gómez's *Mother against the War*, a woman defiantly shields her baby from the call to war.

Depictions of *soldaderas* in Mexican art since the Revolution show them basically as wives and mothers who follow the soldiers and take care of them. Some artists, especially women, have done portraits of famous female fighters, but they are not nearly as numerous as those of male fighters. Women like Érendira, Doña Leona Vicario, and Carmen Serdán are pictured with weapons. The message conveyed by these armed women is of a continuity and a reaffirmation of woman's right to fight for her convictions. But this message is often lost in the more common portrayal of *soldaderas* as nameless, long-suffering, sometimes base female relatives of male soldiers.

Films

Mexican revolutionary cinema, like its counterparts in literature, *corridos*, and art, gave expression to a national consciousness. *Soldaderas* usually appear in films either as part of the revolutionary background or in key roles. Salvador Toscano filmed the 1910 Revolution in many of its phases. His daughter Carmen Toscano edited a version of his film *Memorias de un mexicano*. It has one Zapatista *soldadera* in the footage. Still in the midst of revolutionary violence, the Ministry of War in 1919 produced *Juan Soldado*, which "glorified the exploits of the common soldier and the soldaderas of the Revolution."[57]

Corridos such as "La Adelita," "La Valentina," "Juana Gallo," "La cucaracha," "Marieta," and John Reed's portrait of "Elizabetta" in *Insurgent Mexico* inspired filmmakers in their characterizations of *soldaderas*. Reed's Elizabetta, Azuela's La Pintada and Camilla, and Orozco's *soldaderas* were the basis for the *soldadera* in Sergei Eisenstein's ill-fated 1934 movie, *¡Qué Viva México!* Diego Rivera and Upton Sinclair both made it possible for Eisenstein to carry out the film project. Rivera enticed him with stories about the beauty of Mexico, while Sinclair promised financial backing. Eisenstein and his crew traveled through Mexico filming the land

and its people. The actors were local farmers. He compiled eighty thousand feet of unedited film. Sinclair wanted a better accounting of his money, so he sent Eisenstein a manager. Filming was delayed, and thirteen months into the project, Eisenstein left for the Soviet Union.[58]

The story, divided into six episodes, features a prologue, four novels, and an epilogue. The fourth novel was entitled "Soldadera." It was the story of Pancha, who followed the army, took care of the soldiers, and bore a child. When her soldier consort died, she took up with another soldier until the Revolution ended. Eisenstein saw the camp follower's psychology of "love and sacrifice" for the soldier change to one of emancipation and final happiness.[59] Pancha was symbolically to bring all the warring factions together, much like a mother would promote peace among her children. Unfortunately, Eisenstein never shot any film on this episode.

Sinclair did not share Eisenstein's ideas for this episode. Indeed, he wrote a letter rebuking the filmmaker for his romanticism: "This story makes no difference to the film, certainly not from the point of view of Mexican interest. It was to portray a ragged and barefoot peon army, with a poor pregnant woman carrying a baby on her back, following the soldiers, feeding them and nursing them. I am not able to see how such incidents could be considered necessary to the portrayal of Mexico."[60] Sinclair demonstrated rather graphically how little he understood Mexico. Eisenstein, on the other hand, showed insight about the importance of Mexican women. He noted that "while she made no appearance . . . her influence is as subtle as the Indian's overconquest of the Spaniard."[61] The conflict was resolved when Eisenstein dropped the project and returned to the Soviet Union.

La Adelita (1937) reveals one of the problems of analyzing the role of the *soldaderas* in film. The essentials are there, as Adelita loses her loved ones and fights for justice and revenge. But the focus is more on the melodramatic relations she has with a rich man's son. In this film, one-time director Guillermo Hernández Gómez counts on familiarity with the Adelita *corrido* to attract an audience. *La Valentina* (1938) takes place during the Revolution, but the characters cannot be considered realistic. The two male characters, a general portrayed by Jorge Negrete and a civilian, vie with each other for the affections of a woman named Valentina. The general fights no battles, but wins the heart of Valentina by singing many songs to her. Valentina, played by Esperanza Baur, remains with the general because he respects her and does not try to take her by force. In this way, the film idealistically suggests that proper respect for women comes from the revolutionary experience.[62]

Films made in the 1940s, most notably, *Flor Silvestre* (1943) and *Enamorada* (1946), take place during the Revolution but tend to focus on the relationship between star-crossed lovers. Emilio Fernández directed both films. In *Flor Silvestre* Dolores Del Río plays a rebel's wife who lives through his execution. As befitting her social role as mother, she rears her son to respect his brave, dead father. Missing in this film is what happened to a widow who either fended for herself or followed the troops.

La Enamorada is also about a strong-willed upper-class woman who verbally spars with a rebel general. María Félix and Pedro Armendáriz star. In real life the woman played by Félix would have used her inheritance or asked her father for funds to raise a troop of soldiers (either male or female) and become a *capitana* or a *coronela*. She would have fought in alliance with the rebel general and her outspokenness and veracity would have been incorporated into the general's overall command. Instead, the director ignores realism and settles for fantasy. In the last scene, the rebuffed general is off to war, and the Félix character runs off after him as a camp follower. In this respect, the director imposes his own view about women and their roles in the Revolution.[63]

The casting of María Félix at first glance is perfect for roles about *soldaderas* who are self-willed. Félix is a larger-than-life actress, given to slapping, hitting, kicking and yelling at her male counterparts. Her shrewish characters in many Mexican movies attract and intimidate her male costars. Usually by film's end she has either submitted or rechanneled her vitality into nationalistic sentiments and endeavors. In *La Escondida* (1955) she plays a "bad" woman who forsakes her poor but true Zapatista lover to live with a federal general who gives her many material benefits. In the course of the film, her character shoots the general, reconciles with the Zapatista for a while, and is killed trying to run away from him.

In *La Cucaracha* (1958), Félix plays an officer who is outspoken and, like the character in the *corrido* of the same name, likes men, wine, and fighting. Because she is crude, her true love, a colonel (played by Emilio Fernández), rejects her and links up with a modest widow (played by Dolores Del Río). The colonel likes her gentleness, good manners, and devotion. She never upstages him because she knows her place in relation to him. Félix's character becomes pregnant, however, and having a baby changes her from a wild, out-of-control hothead to a dress-wearing camp follower by film's end.

In 1960 Félix portrayed Juana Gallo in a film loosely based on the life of an officer named María Soledad Ruiz Pérez. Once again she is fearless, a natural leader, but plagued by many men who desire her. She naturally likes the officer who dallies with but does not commit to her, while she ignores the coarse rebel who loves her. By film's end both men are killed. She as "Mother Mexico" is left to ponder her lost lovers and to lead soldiers into the future by rechanneling her energies into nationalistic endeavors. Ruiz Pérez claimed the film was filled with lies. As an officer she never danced or drank with soldiers; such actions would have lessened her authority and the tight discipline female officers generally demanded of their soldiers.[64] Having a relationship with a soldier might have gotten her pregnant and ended her fighting career.

Félix's next portrayal of a *soldadera* was a remake of *La Valentina* (1965). In this film, armed conflict and violence give way to comedy and nostalgia for the Revolution. Félix's character likes guns and ordering her father and brothers around. She has three lovers. She grows to love one of them, and her personality changes into that of a more soft-spoken, fearful woman. This film trivializes the Revolution and the real women who fought in it with its many popular stars, trite dialogue, and tiresome musical numbers.

La Generala (1970) is the last film in which Félix plays an officer. This film was influenced by Fellini and Buñuel in terms of sexual perversion and surrealistically grotesque scenes. Félix's character is prompted into fighting to avenge the cruel death of her brother. She gathers loyal followers and a troop to help her castrate a federal officer, kill other conspirators in her brother's death, and then burn their haciendas to the ground. When she is not wildly rampaging through the haciendas, she allows herself to be wooed by a rich gentleman. In the last scene, she shoots the castrated officer dead before she is killed. Films in which Félix portrays officers are very much off the mark in that not much is made of the real war experiences of women, nor of their personal ideals or their role as officers.

La Soldadera (1966), a film by José Bolaños, was made to counter the Félix depictions of the *soldadera*. Bolaños based his film on Reed's Elizabetta and Eisenstein's ideas about the *soldaderas*. His *soldadera*, Lázara, is played by blonde Silvia Pinal. She does not come from the lowest class but rather from a town and is expected to marry well and live in a fine house. Her new husband is taken away to fight, so she follows him. She finds him dead in the battlefield and from that point on loses her will to live. Like Reed's Elizabetta, she links up with a rebel who orders her to be his woman. After he dies she joins another soldier who cares for her. Lázara seems only to be going through the motions of living. To his credit Bolaños does place this dull, whiny character with other *soldaderas* who are more lively. The good parts of the film deal with the camp and march scenes, where the women are depicted as individuals with different personalities.

Soldaderas have appeared in many forms of Mexican popular culture over the centuries, because so much of the history of Mexico has revolved around wars, revolutions, and armies. Indian, Spanish, and Mexican myths, legends, and novels have their share of Amazon warrior women and camp followers. Since the Revolution, *soldadera* characters have also appeared in murals and films.

Several themes have emerged from these forms of cultural expression, especially that of the remaking of strong-willed female fighters into more feminine and submissive helpmates. Love appears to turn Amazons into docile wives and mothers.

7 *Soldaderas* in Aztlán

The cry for justice originated in the throats of the Adelitas of our yesteryear.

—*Esther Picazo*

Family recollections and social attitudes about the *soldaderas* formed part of the cultural luggage that Mexican immigrants brought with them to the United States. The *soldaderas* continued to be highly visible characters in Chicano literature, art, and discourse. American films about Mexico served to reinforce the view of Mexican women either as well-armed, violent spitfires or barefoot, pregnant, camp follower drudges.

Since the Revolution, Mexicans in the United States have engaged in a redefinition of women's roles in political and cultural struggle. In particular, Chicanas have been affected by the legacy of the *soldaderas*. Chicanas have either identified with aspects of the image or have been offended by the negative perception of the *soldaderas*. There has been a concern among many Chicanas about the appropriateness of the *soldadera* image as a symbol of the Mexican woman. This issue is important to Chicanas because they want to anchor themselves in Mexican culture while expanding their personal horizons beyond that of wife, mother, and defender of La Raza.

For these reasons, Chicanas more than any other group have taken the image of the *soldadera* seriously. Since the 1960s a deluge of materials about Mexicans, Chicanos, and Chicanas has circulated in universities and the media. Much of this material has *soldaderas* as characters. The material can be divided into five general categories: historical accounts (autobiographical/biographical and oral history); fiction (novels, short stories and poetry); the arts; American films; and political essays by Chicanos and Chicanas.

Historical Accounts

There has been a significant and constant influx of Mexicans into the United States since the Revolution. From 1900 to 1930, over one million immigrants entered the country. While most entered through Texas and remained there, thousands settled in Arizona and California. Both former military personnel and civilians fled the constant warfare and economic chaos of the Revolution. The second cycle of immigration began during World War II, highlighted by the Bracero program. The third cycle of large-scale immigration began in 1956 and continues to the present.[1]

Stories about the Revolution form a part of the cultural heritage of the immigrant generation. Implicit in these recollections are sociocultural messages about the *soldaderas* and, consequently, about Mexican women in general. Not surprisingly, some recollections about the *soldaderas* reinforce stereotypes about women as both sexual beings and servants. At the same time, some remembrances express awe, wonder, and some uneasiness about the *soldaderas* who enthusiastically went with soldiers to be either fighters or camp followers.

Many Chicanos trace the entry of their families into the United States to the Revolution. Family sagas reveal personal, political, and economic reasons for leaving Mexico. There is sometimes a striking imbalance between the telling of why men left Mexico and the only sporadic mention of why women left. Ernesto Galarza in his autobiography, *Barrio Boy*, remembers the Revolution as a series of marchers, *soldaderas*, and horsemen. He came into contact with camp followers who cooked, carried rifles, bedrolls, and children on the march. But he indicates that in one uprising, men, women, and children fought together against the *federales*. In particular, Galarza remembers that his mother, like other female villagers and townspeople, let the *soldaderas* use water from their well and "offered a pinch of salt or a pepper or a small lump of corn dough."[2]

In his autobiography Anthony Quinn includes the memoirs of his mother's experience as a *soldadera*. In 1918 the family moved to California and Manuela Oaxaca Quinn worked with her husband on the railroad. She gained her husband's respect as a *soldadera* as well as by sharing this work experience.[3]

Both Lt. "Angel" Jiménez and María Villasana López (profiled in chapter 4) left Mexico to settle in San José, California. Jiménez in particular promoted Mexican cultural pride in the United States and engaged in various kinds of social activism. Her story is a classic portrait of a female soldier. Unfortunately, it has not been widely disseminated in the Chicano media or in anthologies about Mexican women.

The story of the Yniguez family's migration from Mexico appeared in the *Los Angeles Times* as a feature story about Chicanos on July 24, 1983. Among the family's favorite ancestors were "General José Inés Salazar, a colorful rebel leader who is said to have fought on various sides during the Mexican Revolution, and a great-aunt, another revolutionary, said to have ridden a horse better than any man."

Enrique ("Hank") López, a Chicano activist, lawyer, and journalist, has written about his roots in Mexico. Noting the tendency of Chicanos to refer to their "officer" relatives, he claims that his father was "the only private" in the army of Francisco Villa. The two songs he heard as a youth were "La Adelita" and "Se llevaron el cañón para Bachimba."[4] Both songs recall the participation of women in the Revolution. Adalberto Joel Acosta's autobiography, *Chicanos Can Make It*, in contrast to others, refers to the *soldaderas* as loose women and prostitutes. Acosta (born in Santa María de Oro, Durango) recalls that in 1914 Villa came into his town. When he left twenty men joined him along with "three or four of the town's ripest and most experienced whores."[5] It is unclear whether Acosta judges women who volunteered for service to be prostitutes or in fact whether these women were intent on plying their trade with the soldiers.

Enriqueta Longeaux y Vásquez, a Chicana activist from New Mexico, recalls her mother telling her about her experiences in Mexico. When the Villista army went through her village, the men marched "continuously for three days" and the "battalion of women" marched for a whole day. This information confirms the conjecture that *soldaderas* numbered between 20 and 30 percent of many armed groups.[6]

Fiction

Some of the early literature produced by Mexican immigrants or their United States–born children included the *soldaderas*. Just as in the autobiographies, much of this literature is derived from family history reshaped into fictional accounts. Apart from Josephina Niggli's play *Soldadera* (produced in 1936), most of the fictional *soldaderas* created by later authors tend to be one-dimensional and lack an awareness of gender struggles that were waged within the context of the Revolution.

Niggli's work is well developed and complex because as a young girl she lived through the Revolution. Her family emigrated to the United States and she attended the University of North Carolina, where she majored in English and theater arts. She wanted her play to counter the romantic image of the *soldadera* in songs, poetry, and patriotic celebrations. She explores themes such as the brutally repressive nature of the Porfiriato upon women, relationships with men, development of independence, and cynicism about the Revolution.

Because Niggli wanted to show how different the *soldaderas* were from one another, she created seven female characters and only one male. The female followers of Venustiano Carranza include Concha, the leader; María, the sentry; the Blond, an ammunition guard; Cricket, the flirt; two older women named Tomasa and the Old One; and Adelita, the young girl. While guarding a mountain pass and ammunition depot in the Sierra Madre near Saltillo, Coahuila, the *soldaderas* capture a federal spy. The captive, called "The Rich One," tries to talk the women into letting him go or into defecting to the federal ranks of army women.

Niggli shows the measures the Porfiriato used to repress the people. Most of the *soldaderas* in her play have experienced violence against themselves or their loved ones. Concha's father died while attempting to prevent a rich man from raping her. María's husband had his eyes torn out by the *federales*. The Blond saw her husband hanged from the door. Cricket was raped by a rich man at age fourteen. Tomasa watched the *federales* send starving dogs to tear apart her son. The Old One's son was taken by the *federales* and crucified. Adelita's mother died and the other women of the camp had to take her in. From this "spell of common suffering" came the will of these women to fight against the *federales*.[7]

Niggli's *soldaderas* also discuss their relationships with their soldier consorts. Early in the Revolution, the *soldaderas* had fought alongside the men but times had changed. Hilario, the rebel leader, has ordered them to protect the ammunition stores. The Old One considers the order a demotion. She says, "Hilario won't let us fight anymore, but we're good enough to mold his bullets for him, guard his ammo and keep a prisoner." Concha, the leader, shows her annoyance only with the men of the regular army. The captured federal soldier tells her to join them, "as it is a safer life, one in which the federales give women little things they like, such as perfume, jewelry and holy medals." Concha prefers the rebel men because they give her excitement. "I love danger, a sheltered life doesn't mean very much any more."

Concha warns the prisoner that with the men gone, no one can stop the women from torturing him. "There are no men here to tell us what to do. We stand alone. You are merely the victim." The women decide to have a lottery about the best method to torture him to death (male soldiers often held lotteries to determine who would be the first to rape a group of captured women). The women's choices range from crucifixion, spread-eagled on a maguey plant, to staking to the ground and placing red ants all over his body.

The *soldaderas* show their independence in other ways as well. Concha orders the prisoner to take his hat off, as she considers herself "no common soldier's woman." He seems surprised to discover that Concha acts as the main supplier of ammunition and bombs to the rebels. María, the sentry, also shocks him because she shoots him in the shoulder as he tries to escape. On another occasion, the prisoner thinks he can overpower Concha only to discover that Cricket has been covering her from behind some rocks.

Cricket represents a *soldadera* interested in free love. She demands the same rights that men have in the sexual arena. When chided by the other women for frequenting bars in Saltillo, she counters with, "A woman has to have some fun. That soldier of mine isn't wasting his minutes, I can tell you. I've got as many rights as he has." Unfortunately, Cricket believes the prisoner when he tries to bribe her and gives him a mirror with which he signals federal troops. Perhaps Niggli means to suggest that a woman who dwells on sex and has an obsession with trinkets becomes a weak link in the solidarity of a women's group.

The *soldaderas* also question revolutionary ideals. Five of them become involved in the lottery about how to torture the prisoner. For them, the Revolution means exacting revenge against "the rich ones" as represented by the prisoner. Concha and Adelita represent two other views of the Revolution, however. Concha is a hardened, battle-weary soldier who knows that war means destruction. She compares the *soldaderas* and the Revolution itself to fire that rises in flames and destroys everything.

Concha volunteers to save the ammunition stores in a suicide mission in which she would blow herself up along with *federales*. She decides to take the mission, not out of revolutionary fervor, but because as a soldier she must do her duty. Adelita, however, grabs the bomb from her and completes the mission.

Adelita is the uncorrupted *soldadera*. She does not believe in revenge, but in sacrificing her life so her people can live better. She calls the Revolution "beautiful, glorious and heroic" and dies giving all she has "for freedom." Despite the bravery of Adelita, Concha turns to her companions and asks if they are happy about the sacrifice. Niggli ends the play with the *soldaderas* singing "La Adelita," knowing full well that yet again the eternal circle of death and life has been completed.[8]

Writers who did not themselves live through the Revolution tend to create superficial *soldaderas*. Luis M. Valdez, author of the play *Bernabé* (1970) is a case in point. The play is about a mentally and physically disabled farmworker who is transformed into a Chicano after contact with two mythical figures, La Luna, a *pachuco* (gang-oriented youth) dressed in a zoot suit, and La Tierra, a *soldadera* wearing bandoliers. The *pachuco* and the *soldadera* represent Bernabé's male and female aspects. Curiously, it is the *soldadera* who tells him that a Chicano must fight for justice.

The *soldadera* serves as a symbol of an independent and assertive Amazon who will make Bernabé a man. By sleeping with a *soldadera*, he will be transformed into a confident, virile, activist Chicano. In this respect, La Tierra is strictly a sexual being necessary to transform men. At no point does she represent real women and the struggles that female farmworkers, just like *soldaderas*, face in dealing with injustice. For Valdez, La Tierra represents a goddess of war, a fictitious Amazon, a Mexica mythical figure named Cihuacóatl, and a male fantasy.[9]

Roberto J. Garza's 1973 one-act play *On with the Movement* depicts six male characters and one female *soldadera*. They have to decide how best to continue the Mexican Revolution through the Chicano movement. The *soldadera* is portrayed as a sarcastic, loose woman who flirts with all the men. Critical of the men's lack of virility, she relates that the liberation movement needs a "macho." The men do not appreciate her analysis and threaten violence.

They call her "my turtle dove," "some virgin queen," a "wench," an "old hag," and an "old bitch." Clearly, Garza's Chicano movement does not include liberation for Chicanas. Ultimately, the *soldadera* represents a negative image of an activist Chicana in that she seeks a bull among steers who will dominate and tame her. A subliminal message is that once a shrew is tamed, her energies will be redirected into selflessly giving her all to her man and "la Causa." [10]

Ana Montes's one-act play *Adelita* features a poetic recitation at the end. The play's three *soldadera* characters are mothers who are accused by the *federales* of "fighting like men" and "shooting their guns instead of staying home and waiting for their husbands." The action centers on the *federales* forcing one of the *soldaderas*, Adelita, to watch the execution of her son. Adelita asserts that she will shed no tears for her son until the "seeds of freedom" are firmly planted among the people. Once again, the author seems to think that the true *soldadera* finds happiness only when she gives all of her energies to the defense of the people. [11]

The Revolution has also intrigued short story writers. It was used as a link with Chicano activism. Because the Revolution can only be understood in retrospect, short stories say more about current gender struggles than about those waged in 1910. For this reason, the army of men and women depicted in short stories by Carlos G. Vélez-I., Joe L. Navarro, and Roberta Fernández feature *soldaderas* as victims. "The Raid" by Vélez-I. shows women as vulnerable and subject to the good will of men. A mother and her three daughters have to survive different groups of rebels who periodically invade their town. Luck almost runs out on one daughter as a rebel attempts to abduct her and carry her off into the mountains. Her mother tells her she would kill her rather than see her abducted. The matter is resolved by another soldier who orders the man out of the house. It does not seem very likely that the mother would have killed her daughter; it seems more probable that in real life she would have tried to talk the soldier out of the abduction or would have threatened to kill *him*. Such a story shows women only as victims who must depend on protection from men, not from other women. [12]

Navarro's 1972 short story "Stopover at Canacas" depicts *soldaderas* as relatives of male soldiers; he creates one bold female rebel. In this story a rebel commander, Risco, appraises the wounded members of his army. The men are valiant fighters and dedicated to social justice. The women joined his troop because of violence done to their menfolk, or to be near the men. Vera, along with her brother, has been wounded by a grenade in battle. An eighteen-year-old woman has left a convent to fight with a group when she discovers that her father has been killed by government soldiers. She has a wound near the heart. One woman of the troop, Antonia, has lost her husband as well as her mind. None of the *soldaderas* seek revenge for personal injuries done to them. A more balanced story would have shown that *soldaderas* fought to avenge personal injury as well as deadly force leveled against their male relatives.[13]

Roberta Fernández's short story "Zulema" is about a woman who never tells the same tale twice, whether it is about the family or about Mexican folklore. Zulema recalls the tragedy of a *soldadera* named Victoriana. She crosses the border into the safety of the United States in order to wait for her soldier lover, Joaquín. But Joaquín never comes and Victoriana is found thirty years later mummified and still waiting. Zulema changes the story to make it even more romantic and far-fetched and thereby suggests that a *soldadera* (the most brainless of all women) loses her mind when her man dies or leaves her.[14]

Chicanos have written three novels with *soldadera* characters. José Antonio Villarreal's 1959 *Pocho* tells the story of first- and second-generation Mexicans who settled in the United States. He draws a sympathetic portrait of Juan Rubio, a Mexican revolutionary and colonel in Villa's army and the father of Richard ("the Pocho"), the main character. In this story the *soldaderas* act as a threat to the male soldiers. In a conversation between several former soldiers who emigrated to the United States, the story of General Juan Carrillo recalls this threat. Apparently, Carrillo gave his *soldaderas* rifles and taught them how to shoot. Juan Rubio remembers that Carrillo's *soldadera* shot him, "a grown man who allowed his balls to be shot clean away from his body." This story reminds Mexicans that armed, aggressive women always represent danger for men.

While no doubt exists that Juan Rubio served as a soldier, Villarreal remains rather vague about Richard's mother's status. Consuelo Rubio recalls constant train evacuations "because she was Juan Rubio's wife and the people who were coming to take the town were his enemies and would destroy her and her children."[15] Later in the novel Consuelo becomes more assertive toward her husband. Richard alludes to the impact of the more liberal American views about women's rights. But if Consuelo was a *soldadera*, used to living and traveling on her own and being one step from execution, it seems possible that her assertiveness was rooted in her own war experiences in Mexico.

Villarreal's second novel, *The Fifth Horseman*, continues the saga of a Mexican soldier during the Revolution. Villarreal describes the Villista army as a "man-woman army." Heraclio is the main character and the novel details his many affairs and his actions as a Dorado. It portrays Mexican women, many of them *soldaderas*, as primarily sexual beings. The Revolution for these characters means liberation aggressively to seek out sex partners. While many *soldaderas* may have challenged codes of sexual behavior during the Revolution, they also questioned male authority on the battlefields and in the camps.[16]

The first section of Richard Vásquez's novel *Chicano* (1970) dwells on the frightening experiences that Mexicans faced when confronted by waves of *federales* and rebels invading their villages. Both men and women were fearful of the *leva* (draft). Men would be taken as soldiers and women as cooks and consorts. When a rebel group enters a village and asks the villagers to join them, only two persons go with them willingly. One young girl "perhaps fifteen, with pretty flashing eyes, dressed in rags," decides to join them. The rebel leader gives her a lady's riding outfit and a horse, which she can keep as long as she rides with the troop. Shortly after the rebels leave, federal forces come into the village and take five men as recruits. Two young women are relieved that neither of the army conscriptors drafted them. Vásquez's three female characters are not fleshed out, however, and the dialogue about women caught in war is scanty.[17]

For many Chicanas, poetry represents the primary medium of self-expression and means of exploring cultural roots and gender identity. Chicana feminist Ana Nieto Gómez writes in her 1969 poem "Somos Chicanas de Aztlán" that women are *soldaderas* to the men as well as the Adelitas and Juana Gallos of the present day.[18] Sylvia Alicia Gonzales, in "La Chicana," calls La Adelita and La Valentina the inspiration of La Raza. She says that "the Chicano fights for his people; and follows the tradition of Adelita; brown woman, valiant woman."[19] In "Abuelas revolucionarias," María Herrera-Sobek honors grandmothers as "ancient, contrary and bold ladies" who followed their men barefooted to distant lands. Her last verse states that the granddaughters of such women should be committed to valiant actions just like the old ones.[20]

Lorna Dee Cervantes, while not writing directly about the *soldaderas'* legacy, does use imagery that suggests it. In her poem "Beneath the Shadow of the Freeway," she calls her family "a woman family," composed of Grandma, the "innocent Queen," and her mother, "the swift knight, fearless warrior."[21]

Gloria Pérez revels in expressing her unity with the Chicano. In her poem "Mi hombre," she presents a distinctly sexual unification by comparing the Chicano to "the sumptuous pyramids of Tenochtitlan." The Chicano stands in her mind "erect; like la Adelita, always at the side of the guerrilla."[22]

Ana Nieto Gómez was one of the first Chicanas to question the view of the *soldaderas* as strictly defenders of La Raza. In her poem "Youth I Mirror," she mentions that female soldiers had to disguise themselves to fight in the ranks by cutting their hair and changing their names from Juana to Juan and Petra to Pedro. Unlike the *soldaderas*, who equated fighting with a male role, many Chicanas like Nieto Gómez in the 1970s believed fighting not to be gender-specific.[23] This poem reflects Chicana assertiveness in questioning why they had to submerge themselves and women's issues and concentrate only on race and class struggles.

The Arts

In the arts, Chicanas have insisted that dances featuring the *soldaderas* be incorporated into Chicano repertory companies. Folk dances like "Las Adelitas" and "La Jesusita en Chihuahua" have proved to be great favorites in Chicano festivals. "Las Adelitas" is performed only by women. To the sounds of a coronet playing a march and a snare drum playing a military beat, twenty women act out many common military movements. They march with rifles on their shoulders, then kneel on one knee and aim the rifles at the audience, which represents the enemy. Similarly, only women perform "La Jesusita en Chihuahua." They wear a belt of bullets across the chest but do not carry rifles. The dance also has livelier movements, such as hops, running heel-toe steps, and movement of the full skirt.[24]

Soldaderas also appear in many murals that grace barrio walls throughout the Southwest. One of the first murals to be painted, *Untitled* (1968) by Antonio Bernal, in Del Rey, California, is unique in its warrior-women portrayals. One side of the wall depicts pre-

Conquest Indians. Leading them is a Mexica woman who can be taken for an *auianime* or a *mociuaquetzque*. On the other side of the wall a *soldadera* with drawn machete leads a variety of Mexican, Chicano, and African-American heroes.

While this and other murals show realistic *soldaderas*, other muralists tend to emphasize women's sexuality. The *La Adelita* mural (1976) at Ramona Gardens, Los Angeles, painted by Carlos Almaraz and Los Four, exemplifies this tendency. In this mural, subtitled *Mother of the Land and Liberty*, a *soldadera* kneels on one knee with a rifle in her hands. Her rebozo does little to hide her enormous breasts.[25]

Chicana artists have tried to counter this image and others that depict *soldaderas* topless, wearing low-cut blouses, breast-feeding, or with hair flowing freely in the wind. Santa Barraza, a Chicana artist from Texas, has done pencil drawings of *soldaderas* in *Adelita* and *Soldaderas jóvenes*. She sketches children to show that *soldaderas*, since early youth, fought for their identity as women and Mexicans. Carmen Rodríguez has painted a *soldadera* mother wearing a bandolier and carrying a baby who is sucking on a bullet cartridge pacifier.[26]

American Films

American films have served to reinforce cultural stereotypes about Mexican women and *soldaderas* as background scenery, submissive servants, and erotic beings. The influence of these films on Chicanas and Chicanos cannot be underestimated. American films that have *soldadera* characters are not just about the Revolution but also about army women during the Texas Revolution (1836) and the French Intervention (1860).

John Wayne's extravagant film *The Alamo* (1960) tells the story of the Texas Revolution. During the attack on the Alamo by Mexican soldiers, American fighters like Davy Crockett, Jim Bowie, and William Travis die. Two scenes focus on silent *soldaderas*, who constitute part of the exotic background during the conflict. After the battle, *soldaderas* appear to remove the dead and wounded Mexican soldiers from the battlefield. At the end of the film, a white woman and child leave the Alamo. As they depart *soldaderas* are shown making the sign of the cross, as if to indicate the holy and heroic sacrifice of the dead Americans and the survivors.

Set in Mexico during the French Intervention, the movie *Vera*

Cruz (1954) stars Gary Cooper and Sarita Montiel. A group of American adventurers agree to escort a French woman and gold to the port of Vera Cruz. Blocking their path are the rebel soldiers of Benito Juárez. A Mexican female rebel spy infiltrates the American camp and establishes a relationship with Gary Cooper. She is naturally very attractive, excellent with horses, a wagon driver, and a patriot. By the end of the film she has convinced Cooper to give the gold to the rebels.

American films that deal with the Mexican Revolution and feature *soldadera* characters are *Viva Villa* (1934), *Viva Zapata* (1952), *The Wild Bunch* (1969), and *The Professionals* (1969). In *Viva Villa*, *soldaderas*, riding on horseback and wearing bandoliers, are pictured only during a victory scene for Villa's army. This scene, however, was actual live footage from one of Villa's campaigns.

Viva Zapata is the one film that shows numerous scenes of the army of men and women. Zapatista men and women work together to free Zapata, to derail a *federales* train, to celebrate victories together, and to keep rifles handy for unexpected attacks. A crucial scene of the army in action takes place when the Zapatistas have a *federales* fort under siege. It is the women, loaded with food baskets containing dynamite, who approach the fort first.

Under the pretense of selling food, the women pile the baskets at the main gate. Facing enemy fire, several *soldaderas*, under orders from another woman, rush the gate with torches to set off the dynamite baskets. Even though some are killed, others pick up the torches and keep rushing the gate until the explosives are set off. Only at this point does the Zapatista cavalry rush into the fort to finish off the *federales*. This is an excellent depiction of how a male and female army operated in unison to defeat a common enemy. The scene's accuracy is due in no small part to screenwriter John Steinbeck's interviews with Zapatista veterans.[27]

While the film accurately shows women in battle, their reasons for fighting are not presented. Grievances against the Porfirian tyranny are noted in the film, but little is made of the abuses women endured at the hands of the *federales*, ranging from rape to abduction to murder of loved ones to starvation tactics used to drive the people from their land. In addition, throughout all of these scenes, most of the *soldaderas* remain silent observers, with few speaking parts and expressing little curiosity or criticism about Zapatista strategies to defeat the *federales*. Margo (Albert) plays the most talkative *soldadera*. She is in fact called "*soldadera*." She appeared to be at Zapata's side at some key points, but only as a listener.

Unlike other characters, she never argues with Zapata—even when he kills her husband for being a traitor.

While *Viva Zapata* does not have any American characters, *The Wild Bunch* and *The Professionals* feature American soldiers of fortune in key parts, despite the fact that few American mercenaries dared to stay very long among Mexican rebels who were only too happy to send them home in coffins. The interjection of American male characters makes these films less about the Revolution and more like other Westerns. In this context, *soldaderas* resemble frontier prostitutes or the "dark, exotic, foreign, quasi-masculine" women who fight with or against men sometimes and make passionate love to them at all other times.[28]

The *Wild Bunch* has an all-star cast. Made by Sam Peckinpah, the movie is violent and bloody, with virile men and either oversexed *soldaderas* or silent tortilla-making drudges at the campsites. The Mexican character Angel kills his traitorous former girlfriend Teresa after she does the unforgivable and becomes the *soldadera* for the cruel General Mapache. What she gains from the relationship with Mapache is food, clothing, and money. Angel shoots Teresa for betraying him, thereby reaffirming the double standard.

In *The Professionals*, the portrayal of a female Villista is sheer fantasy and an almost complete misrepresentation of historical accounts of female fighters. Film critic Arthur G. Pettit idealizes the female character as the key player in turning the mercenary American soldiers into moral human beings.[29] But how can anyone take a character seriously whose name is Lt. Sí, Sí, Chiquita? The adventurers first see Chiquita participating in a rebel attack on a train. The next sighting takes place when Chiquita (bare from the waist up) is washing herself.

The dialogue is equally sex-charged. She is described as a woman who never says no. Before the conclusion of the film, Chiquita (played by María Gómez) and the American character (played by Burt Lancaster) have the following conversation:

> B.L.: Chiquita, how's your love life?
> M.G.: Terrific. You want some?
> B.L.: Don't you ever say no?
> M.G.: Never!
> B.L.: Anybody?
> M.G.: Everybody.

In subsequent action, he shoots Chiquita as she tries to protect her leader. As she lies dying, she tries to shoot him, but as Hollywood and luck would have it, the gun has no more bullets. Bill (Lancaster) then tells Chiquita she is beautiful and kisses her farewell.

This characterization is not substantiated by historical accounts. Most female fighters made it clear to their fellow soldiers that any amorous advances would bring about a violent response. They were fighters and activities that got them pregnant and out of action were frowned on.

Soldaderas often appear in American films about Mexican wars (e.g., *Vera Cruz, The Wild Bunch,* and *The Professionals*). Army women are part of the background—as bystanders, girlfriends, and wives of the soldiers—in these films. Sometimes women display war prowess or intelligence, but these qualities are diminished considerably by the sexy clothes they wear and the whorish banter they engage in. American men in some of these films dally with *soldadera* "dark ladies" or "Mexican spitfires" and let loose their sexual and romantic fantasies.

Political Essays by Chicanos and Chicanas

Just as varying images of the *soldaderas* appear in Chicano literature and American movies, so too do women and men use the image in the political rhetoric of the Chicano movement. The *soldadera* image was initially used by Chicano civil rights groups to recruit female members. Many activists used the diminutive "Las Adelitas" to refer to Chicanas. In some instances, the use of the *soldadera* image seemed part of Chicano fascination with Mexican revolutionaries like Pancho Villa and Emiliano Zapata, as well as an expression of intergroup solidarity. Chicanos and Chicanas were urged to fight, just like their ancestors, against the common foes of racism and classism. Gender inequities were not addressed initially by the movement.

"Mujeres valientes," with words by Miguel Barragán, is a popular *corrido* in the Farmworkers' movement. The *corrido* urges women to go out into the "battlefields of liberation." The words proclaim that there are women who fight, "they are the Adelitas, beautiful Chicanas . . . of the Revolution." Often female farmworkers psyche themselves up for picket duty by comparing themselves to Adelitas. The Mexican-American Youth Organization (MAYO), a campus organization, tried to attract women by comparing Chicana students to las Adelitas. Another more militant group, the Brown Berets, who dressed in paramilitary garb, unofficially called women members "Adelitas."[30]

In *Chicano Manifesto*, Armando R. Rendón notes that men and women have different views about calling Chicanas "*soldaderas*":

> A struggle is going on between our women and men. . . . The
> women are saying that they want to be recognized by the Chicano
> macho as a companion in the revolution. . . . Young girls are relat-
> ing to the folk heroines of the Mexican Revolution—La Adelita,
> subject of a revolutionary corrido, who exemplified the soldaderas
> . . . it probably will avail los machos nothing to reject las mujeres
> who are insisting on becoming revolutionaries; they will do so in
> spite of opposition. . . . I suspect that the Chicano revolt, in all its
> phases and efforts, will have to draw upon the indomitable energy
> and commitment to the Chicano family of la mujer de la raza.[31]

Rendón supports Chicana revolutionaries as long as defense and survival of men and the family are the concerns of women.

David F. Gómez in *Somos Chicanos* (1973) notes that without the help of the Adelitas the Revolution would have been lost. In similar fashion Gómez tells Chicanos that a war is being waged for civil rights and the men need women to join the battle.[32]

Chicano activists used the diminutive "Las Adelitas" to refer to Chicanas for a number of reasons. Carlos Vásquez claims that the romantic qualities of Las Adelitas were encouraged as an excellent way to keep women "quiet and obedient."[33] While some Chicanos called women their revolutionary sisters, Evangelina Enríquez and Alfredo Mirande note that this often implied that Chicanas were to do the menial work of the movement. Chicana activists were thought to function best in a Chicano organization as sexual partners of the men, cooks, baby sitters, and clerical helpers.[34]

Chicano activists' attitudes about women were contested by Chicanas. Gema Matsuda, writing for the *Comisión Femenil Mexicana Newsletter*, argued that any Chicana who desired to "partici-pate in the liberation of her people, must then be a very strong character or limit herself to the role of a soldadera."[35] In this con-text, Matsuda displays a narrow understanding of the *soldaderas* as merely camp followers, drudges, and loose women. A broader view would show that some army women were strong, proud, strict, and moral while others were just the opposite. Masuda's limited view is a common one and clouds polemics about the appropriateness of the *soldaderas* as Chicana symbols. The *soldadera* image has been rejected by Chicanas who thought them too subservient and too traditional for the later half of the twentieth century. Velma Villa Romo, in *Comadre*, a Chicano journal, says that the *soldaderas*, although idealized in Mexican culture, were in reality miserable camp followers who did the menial work in the camps and battlefields.[36] Adelaida R. Del Castillo, another Chicana activist, thinks the *soldaderas* were too "masculinized" and did not act out of their own convictions.[37] Norma Cantú at the 1984 National Association of Chicano Studies Conference (NACS) lamented what she called "the Adelita complex" in universities, especially in Chicano studies departments. Its symptoms were the degradation and designation of Chicana studies as a subtopic rather than a core component of Chicano studies. Cantú thought that the widespread belief among Mexican Americans that all women were "Adelitas," or camp followers, was the reason that Chicanos treated Chicana studies as unnecessary and subject to elimination from course offerings.[38]

Other Chicana essayists use *soldadera* imagery to distinguish Mexican and Chicana feminism from Euro-American culture and the women's movement. Martha P. Cotera's classic statement on this point asserts that Chicanas "have a long, beautiful history of Mexicano and Chicano feminism which is not Anglo-inspired, or oriented."[39] She cites the names of many Mexicanas honored as goddesses, queens, and warriors.

Isabelle Navar connects the image of the Mexican woman to the *soldaderas*. In her view, the *soldaderas* had an enduring quality and strength in "conserving and furthering human existence."[40] Enriqueta Longeaux y Vásquez says, "La Adelita" symbolizes the revolutionary woman with the crossed rebozo over her bosom.[41]

Jennie Chávez, in an essay for *Mademoiselle* in April 1972 calls Chicanas "reincarnations" of the Adelitas and Valentinas. Chávez warns Chicanos to value Chicana fighters or to face the subversion of the people's betterment.[42] Esther Picazo, a medical student in 1973, deplored the transition of Mexicans into Mexican Americans and the forsaking of the "Adelitas" for the "Anns" of Anglicized society.[43] Another student, María Terán, said that Chicanas were "Adelita Chicanas" and "true soldadas," as opposed to American "concerned white liberal" women.[44]

Soldadera Images in the 1980s

The most recent use of *soldadera* imagery is found in Luis Valdez's stage presentation of *Corridos* (1983) and Linda Ronstadt's show, *Canciones de mi padre* (1988). In *Corridos* Valdez chooses the *corrido* "La rielera" to tell the story of the women of the Revolution. In "La rielera" the *soldadera* follows her soldier consort on the train in order to cook for him. Valdez says he selected this *corrido* because, where he comes from, "the idea of a woman who went out and cooked for her man on the battlefields reminds me of the campesina woman who goes out and works with her man and still cooks. I think that it is a tribute to the power and strength of the Mexican woman, not to her oppression."[45] This statement was received with great trepidation by Chicanas who were looking for artists and scholars to bring a fresh understanding of the *soldaderas*. Valdez's old-fashioned analysis seemed a step backward.

Valdez's views of other *soldaderas* come from the *corridos*. He thinks that "La Adelita" is about a woman who was "crazily in love with a sargento and was praised by the coronel for being valiant." "La Valentina" describes "just some guy lusting after her." "Juana Gallo" "didn't contain enough to dramatize." As a result, the production features *corridos* of "old-fashioned love tragedies with a macho viewpoint."[46] Valdez uses John Reed as spokesman for the *soldadera* piece, in spite of the fact that Reed's stories are questionable at best. It also seems strange that Reed's observations would be preferred over those of female and male veterans of the Revolution who are still alive. The *soldaderas* in the play, Valentina, Adelita, and La Rielera, talk about "the finding and losing of men, about following men, about holding on to men."[47]

A more stinging Chicana criticism of *Corridos* conveys a sadness about Valdez's use of stereotypes. Katharine A. Díaz, then editor of *Caminos*, wrote with disappointment in her review of *Corridos:*

> I had hoped that the scene depicting the soldaderas would be our salvation. I was disappointed. La Rielera who valiantly follows her man into the war—to fix his meals, *hechar* his tortillas—is rendered virtually helpless upon his death, until another soldier, any soldier, fills his place. Another soldadera, a colonel, is supposed to exhibit the characteristics of an "hembra" the female equivalent of a "macho." She imitates men so much in her actions, though, that I'd say she's macha.[48]

Díaz's statement is typical of those of Chicanas who still seek to understand the *soldaderas* as they really were in Mexican history. The accuracy and dissemination of such knowledge is important to Chicanas because they feel influenced in many ways by the pervasiveness of the image in Mexican and Chicano culture.

Linda Ronstadt's Public Broadcasting System show "Canciones de mi padre" has not increased knowledge about the *soldaderas*. Her rendition of "La rielera" is charming, complete with male and female soldiers, but unenlightening. Her audience still wonders about who the "mysterious" and ever-present *soldaderas* were.

While the *soldaderas* are a part of Mexican history, they have also become a part of Chicano history, because many Mexican immigrants to the United States fled the destructiveness and chaos of the Revolution and subsequent economic crises as well. They brought with them remembrances and culturally reconstructed images of the *soldaderas*. Because the *soldadera* image was largely about assertive or passive women, Chicanas more than other groups have felt challenged or offended by the symbol. It is Chicanas who persistently debate the consequences of the image on their own developing ideas of cultural integrity and women's rights to pursue individual goals.

Conclusion

Soldaderas have marched through most of Mexican history. Their impact on Mexican-style warfare has been immense. Like soldiers in any army, they came from all classes and races. They had different personalities and varying martial skills. This study has questioned and found unsubstantiated the social supposition that men alone are warriors and women are mothers. Due to the large number of rebellions and armed conflicts in Mexico, women's experiences as mothers/warriors have been continual and constantly acknowledged by the larger society in many of its cultural expressions. In religion, the mother/warrior concept has been deified as Our Lady of Guadalupe/María Insurgente.

The word *soldadera* came with the Spanish conquistadors in the Conquest of Mexico (1519). However, the practice of having Mesoamerican and Spanish-European women fighting in battles or following troops was already well established in this hemisphere, in the form of the *mociuaquetzque*. This unarmed woman accompanied a warrior into battle not as a fighter but as a strategist or coach. Malintzin (Doña Marina) in her role as adviser to Hernán Cortés is the best example of a *mociuaquetzque*. The essential duty the *soldadera* (as defined by the Spaniards) performed for the soldier was to take his pay (*soldada*) and buy him food and other supplies.

The soldier, then, was an employer. He hired the *soldadera* to fulfill his needs, necessary because Mexican armies did not provide commissary services until well into the 1920s. To gain the business of the soldier, the *soldadera* would at times have to be aggressive. Like servants everywhere, she could leave one soldier-employer for another at will for a variety of reasons. Similarly, soldiers could cease handing over their wages to one *soldadera* if another offered them a better deal. Some literature, however, gives the impression that all *soldaderas* were strictly female relatives of the soldiers, or were abducted in wartime with few or no options. It also claims that many *soldaderas* followed soldiers out of love or familial loyalty rather than for economic opportunity.

The *soldaderas* were unofficially recognized as a necessary part of the Mexican army. Many of their duties consisted of foraging, cooking, carrying supplies, nursing, sanitary services, spying, gun running, and fighting when necessary. The Mexican army recognized that these services helped to stem the tide of desertions. Despite these key services, however, military rhetoric and practice marginalized the *soldaderas* by placing them at the bottom of the military pecking order.

When the army needed their services, the *soldaderas* stayed in the ranks, and their actions many times were considered awesome and morale inspiring. But at other times, they were abandoned without much hesitation or ordered not to advance with the men into battle. The military was not above calling the *soldaderas* parasites waiting to prey on soldiers. Officers accused them of being whores and of spreading immorality and vice among the soldiers. In fact, General Joaquín Amaro cited just these reasons for cashiering the *soldaderas* from the barracks in 1925.

Mexican women who serve in the armed forces now are called "*soldadas*" rather than "*soldaderas*." Limited opportunities for women in the military have opened up in different units, and, just as in the United States, women go to military academies for officer training. Participation in combat is not really an issue in Mexico, because the army currently exists as a constabulary force.

While the *soldadera* "system" ceased to exist by the 1930s, the cultural legacy of these women has never dissipated. *Soldadera* characters have appeared in most forms of Mexican artistic endeavor. The cultural reconstructions of the *soldaderas* have reflected extremes between the fierce fighter (Juana Gallo) and the base camp follower (La Cucaracha). The "middle ground" *soldadera* character in the person of "La Adelita" has emerged as the clear favorite of artists and writers. "La Adelita" is the "sweetheart of the troops," a woman who is valiant, pretty, and a wonderful helpmate to the soldier.

At first glance, it might seem unlikely that Mexicans who immigrated to the United States would have taken an interest in *soldadera* imagery. But the struggle of Chicanos in the United States has often been perceived as a war requiring that all male and female Mexicans help fight for cultural integrity and civil rights. In another sense, nostalgic adoption by Chicanos and Chicanas of Mexican heroes and heroines for cultural sustenance helps rekindle interest in these symbols.

But far too often it seems to Chicanas that Chicano use of *soldadera* imagery is restricted to nonleadership and auxiliary camp follower roles. Under this presumption, Chicana activists, like *soldaderas*, were to be the sexual companions and clerical helpers of Chicano revolutionaries fighting racial, class—but not gender—injustice. For this reason, some women object to *soldadera* imagery and consider the symbol to be an albatross around the neck. To them *soldadera* imagery is past history that cannot be recycled for modern times. Other Chicanas think that *soldadera* imagery is a powerful legacy and a flexible enough symbol to empower Mexican women for many generations to come. The continuation of the *soldadera* image, whether in Mexico or in the Chicano communities of the United States, suggests that there are battles still to be fought to gain full rights for all of the Mexican people.

Notes

Introduction

1. Other names are *mociuaquetzque* (valiant women), *auianime* (pleasure girls), *capitanas, soldadas,* Juanas, *cucarachas* (cockroaches), *guachas, viejas* (old ladies), and *galletas* (cookies).

2. I use Mexican American and Chicano(a) interchangeably to designate persons born in the United States.

1. Mesoamerican Origins

1. Miguel León-Portilla, *Aztec Thought and Culture,* p. 98.

2. Guadalupe may derive from Coatl (snake) and u Pechack ma (stepped on). Guadalupe was also the name of a Blessed Mother figure in Spain.

3. Don Fernando de Alva Ixtlilxochitl, *Historia chichimeca,* cited in Jacques Soustelle, *Daily Life of the Aztecs on the Eve of the Spanish Conquest,* p. 29.

4. Eric R. Wolf, *Sons of the Shaking Earth,* p. 57.

5. Ibid.

6. Burr C. Brundage, *The Fifth Sun: Aztec Gods, Aztec World,* p. 155; Fray Diego Durán, *The Aztecs: The History of the Indies of New Spain,* pp. 245–246.

7. Brundage, *The Fifth Sun,* pp. 171–173, 244.

8. Frederick Alvin Peterson, "Women Warriors and Laughing Faces," *Natural History* 63 (May 1954): 215.

9. June Nash, "The Aztecs and the Ideology of Male Dominance," *Signs* 4 (Winter 1978): 353.

10. María Sten, *The Mexican Codices and Their Extraordinary History.*

11. Ferdinand Anton, *La mujer en la América antigua*, pp. 62–63.

12. Brundage, *The Fifth Sun*, pp. 135–136.

13. Ibid., p. 136.

14. Adela Formoso de Obregón Santacilia, *La mujer mexicana en la organización social del país*, p. 9.

15. Laurette Sejourne, *Burning Water: Thought and Religion in Ancient Mexico*, p. 19.

16. Fernando Alvarado Tezozomoc, "The Finding and Founding of Tenochtitlán from the Crónica Mexicayotl (1609)," trans. Thelma D. Sullivan, *Tlalocan* 6, no. 4 (1971): 315–316.

17. Ibid.

18. Fray Bernardino de Sahagún, *Florentine Codex, General History of the Things of New Spain*, bk. 2, p. 236.

19. Fernando Horcasitas and Douglas Butterworth, "La Llorona," *Tlalocan* 4 (1963): pp. 208–209.

20. Ibid.

21. León-Portilla, *Aztec Thought and Culture*, pp. 32, 98, 110–111; Durán, *The Aztecs*, p. 230.

22. Fray Juan de Torquemada, *Monarquía indiana*, p. 299. Torquemada called them "maqui."

23. Frances Gillmor, *The King Danced in the Marketplace*, p. 72; Soustelle, *Daily Life of the Aztecs*, pp. 190–191.

24. Edward Kissam and Michael Schmidt, trans., *Poems of the Aztec Peoples*, p. 136.

25. Curt Muser, *Facts and Artifacts of Ancient Middle America*, p. 32.

26. Soustelle, *Daily Life of the Aztecs*, pp. 190–191.

27. Fray Diego Durán, *Book of the Gods and Rites and the Ancient Calendar*, p. 229; Soustelle, *Daily Life of the Aztecs*, pp. 190–191.

28. Durán, *The Aztecs*, pp. 245–246.

29. Ibid., p. 159.

30. Ibid., p. 106.

31. Ross Hassig, *Aztec Warfare: Imperial Expansion and Political Control*, p. 284; Nash, "The Aztecs," p. 358; Durán, *The Aztecs*, pp. 172, 218.

32. Burr Cartwright Brundage, *A Rain of Darts: The Mexica Aztecs*, p. 205.

33. C. A. Burland, *Montezuma, Lord of the Aztecs*, p. 83.

34. Soustelle, *Daily Life of the Aztecs*, p. 179.

35. Durán, *Book of the Gods*, p. 298.

36. Ibid.

37. Sahagún, *Florentine Codex*, bk. 10, p. 12.

38. Durán, *Book of the Gods*, p. 298.

39. Soustelle, *Daily Life of the Aztecs*, p. 184.

40. Ibid., p. 46.

41. Frederick Peterson, *Ancient Mexico: An Introduction to the Pre-Hispanic Cultures*, p. 158. Hassig, *Aztec Warfare*, p. 287, states incorrectly that women did not accompany the Mexica armies.

2. Servants, Traitors, and Heroines

1. Irene L. Plunket, *Isabel of Castile and the Making of the Spanish Nation, 1451–1504*, p. 191.

2. William H. Prescott, *The Portable Prescott: Rise and Decline of the Spanish Empire*, p. 86.

3. Plunket, *Isabel of Castile*, pp. 192, 194–195.

4. Patricia de Fuentes (ed. and trans.), *The Conquistadors: First Person Accounts of the Conquest of Mexico*, p. 232.

5. Antonio de Herrera y Tordesillas, *The General History of the Vast Continent and Islands of America*, vol. 3, p. 168.

6. Ibid., p. 170.

7. Ibid., p. 168; Lamberto Armijo, "Our Early Women—A Profile," *La Luz*, October–November 1979, p. 7.

8. Durán, *The Aztecs*, pp. 321–322.

9. Hubert H. Bancroft, *History of Mexico* vol. 2, pp. 503–504.

10. "La Malinche," in *Enciclopedia de México*, vol. 8 (1972), p. 234; Cordelia Candelaria, "La Malinche, Feminist Prototype," *Frontiers* 5 (Summer 1980): 3.

11. Candelaria, "La Malinche," p. 3.

12. Bernal Díaz del Castillo, *The Conquest of New Spain*, p. 172.

13. J. Jesús Figueroa Torres, *Doña Marina: una india ejemplar*, p. 90; Henry R. Wagner, *The Rise of Fernando Cortés*, pp. 69, 77.

14. Henry C. Gardiner, *Martín López: Conquistador Citizen of Mexico*, p. 134.

15. Robert Anderson Wilson, *A New History of the Conquest of Mexico*, pp. 326–327.

16. Octavio Paz, *The Labyrinth of Solitude: Life and Thought in Mexico*, p. 79.

17. Díaz del Castillo, *The Conquest of New Spain*, p. 395.

18. Durán, *The Aztecs*, pp. 315–316.

19. Prescott, *The Portable Prescott*, p. 279.

20. Miguel León-Portilla (ed.), *The Broken Spears: The Aztec Account of the Conquest of Mexico*, p. 84.

21. Augusto Sisto, *Mitos y leyendas mexicanos*, pp. 143–153; Robert Decker and Esther T. Márquez, *The Proud Mexicans*, pp. 23–25.

22. Philip Wayne Powell, *Soldiers, Indians and Silver: The Northward Advance of New Spain, 1550–1600*, pp. 43, 46.

23. Harry Prescott Johnson, "Diego Martínez de Hurdaide: Defender of the Northwestern Frontier of New Spain," *Pacific Historical Review* 11, no. 2 (June 1942): 182–185.

24. Herbert E. Bolton, *Coronado: Knight of Pueblos and Plains*, p. 62.

25. Ibid.

26. Ibid.

27. Ibid., pp. 76, 117, 238, 377.

28. Ibid., pp. 335, 337.

29. Ibid., p. 332.

30. Fray Angélico Chávez, *My Penitente Land*, p. 46.

31. Gaspar Pérez de Villagra, *History of New Mexico, 1610*, p. 224.

32. *Expedition into New Mexico Made by Antonio de Espejo, 1582–1583 as Revealed in the Journal of Diego Pérez de Luxán, a Member of the Party*, pp. 112–114.

33. Albert H. Schroeder and Dan S. Matson, *A Colony on the Move: Gaspar Castaño de Sosa's Journal, 1590–1591*, pp. 82, 84, 87.

34. Cheryl J. Foote and Sandra K. Schackel, "Indian Women of New Mexico, 1535–1680," in *New Mexico Women: Intercultural Perspectives*, ed. Joan Jensen and Darlis A. Miller, p. 30.

35. Edgar F. Love, "Negro Resistance to Spanish Rule in Colonial Mexico," *Journal of Negro History* 52 (April 1967): 98.

36. Colin A. Palmer, *Slaves of the White God: Blacks in Mexico, 1570–1650*, p. 139. La Mulatta de Córdoba is a folk story of African women in Mexico who resisted slavery and came before the Inquisition.

37. Colin M. MacLachlan and Jaime E. Rodríguez O, *The Forging of the Cosmic Race*, p. 207.

38. Bancroft, *History of Mexico, 1600–1803*, vol. 3, p. 329.

39. John Philip Langellier and Katherine Meyers Peterson, "Lancers and Leather Jackets: Presidial Forces in Spanish Alta California, 1769–1821," *Journal of the West* 20 (October 1981): 8.

40. Donald E. Smith, *The Viceroy of New Spain*, p. 184.

41. Ibid.

42. Catalina de Erauzú, *Historia de la monja alférez*, pp. 1, 119. See also MacLachlan and Rodríguez O., *The Forging of the Cosmic Race*, pp. 239–240; Luis González Obregón, *The Streets of Mexico*, pp. 153–157.

43. González Obregón, *The Streets of Mexico*, p. 155.

44. Ibid.

45. Ibid., p. 156.

46. Ibid.

47. Philip E. Lampe, "Our Lady of Guadalupe and Ethnic Prejudice," *Borderlands Journal* 9, no. 1 (Spring 1986): 96.

48. Matt S. Meier, "María Insurgente," *Historia Mexicana* 23 (1973): 471.

49. Ibid.

50. Jacques Lafaye, *Quetzalcoatl and Guadalupe: The Formation of Mexican National Consciousness, 1531–1813*, p. xix.

51. Murray L. Wax, *Indian Americans: Unity and Diversity*, p. 12.

52. Luis González Obregón, *Episodios de la guerra de independencia*, p. 74.

53. Mario Salcedo Guerrero, "Vicente Guerrero's Struggle for Mexican Independence, 1810–1821," p. 51.

54. John Anthony Caruso, *The Liberators of Mexico*, p. 12.

55. Otilia Arosemena de Tejeira, "The Woman in Latin America: Past, Present, Future," *Americas* 26 (April 1974): S-6.

56. Silvia Marina Arrom, *The Women of Mexico City, 1790–1857*, p. 32.

57. Ibid., p. 34.

58. Carlos Hernández, *Mujeres célebres de México*, p. 144.

59. Arrom, *The Women of Mexico City,* p. 37.

60. Ibid., p. 38.

61. Ibid., pp. 40, 41.

62. Ibid., p. 33.

63. Ibid., p. 35.

64. Martha P. Cotera, *Diosa y hembra: The History and Heritage of Chicanas in the United States,* p. 39.

65. Ramón Eduardo Ruiz, *The Mexican War: Was It Manifest Destiny?,* p. 1.

66. Richard G. Santos, *Santa Anna's Campaign against Texas, 1835– 1836,* p. 17.

67. James T. DeShields, *Tall Men with Long Rifles,* pp. 102–103.

68. De la Peña, *With Santa Anna in Texas,* p. 190.

69. Ibid., p. xxi.

70. J. Hefter (ed.), *El soldado mexicano; organización, vestuario, equipo. The Mexican Soldier; organization, dress, equipment, 1837–1847,* p. 22.

71. Lester Hamilton, *Goliad Survivor: Isaac D. Hamilton,* p. 47.

72. Ibid., pp. 48–49, 63–64, 66–67.

73. Frances Calderón de la Barca, *Life in Mexico,* pp. 433–434.

74. George Winston Smith and Charles Judah, eds., *Chronicles of the Gringos: The U.S. Army in the Mexican War, 1846–1848,* p. 90; quotation from Robert W. Johannsen, *To the Halls of the Montezumas: The Mexican War in the American Imagination,* p. 137.

75. Ricardo Romero Aceves, *La mujer en la historia de México,* pp. 170–172.

76. Michael C. Meyer and William L. Sherman, *The Course of Mexican History,* p. 346.

77. Anna Nieto-Gómez, "Women in Mexican History: Cinco de Mayo," p. 17.

78. Smith and Judah, *Chronicles of the Gringos,* p. 216.

79. Samuel E. Chamberlain, *My Confession,* pp. 213–214.

80. Ibid., pp. 210–217.

81. Maurice Garland Fulton (ed.), *Diary and Letters of Josiah Gregg: Excursions in Mexico and California, 1847–1850,* p. 117.

82. Smith and Judah, *Chronicles of the Gringos,* p. 308.

83. Adelina Zendejas, *La mujer en la intervención francesa,* p. 81.

84. Antonio Uroz, *Hombres y mujeres de México,* pp. 261–262.

85. Nieto-Gómez, "Women in Mexican History," p. 17.

86. Luis Leal, *Aztlán y México: Perfiles literarios e históricos,* p. 185.

87. Ibid.

88. Romero-Aceves, *La mujer en la historia de México,* pp. 187–190.

89. Angel Salas, "La batalla del 5 de mayo en el Peñón," *Mexican Folkways* 8, no. 2 (April–June 1833): 61.

90. Charles Lemprière, *Notes in Mexico in 1861 and 1862,* p. 360.

91. Jack Autrey Dabbs, *The French Army in Mexico, 1861–1867: A Study of Military Government,* p. 258.

92. Eleanor Hague, *Spanish-American Folk-Songs,* pp. 107–108.

3. Amazons and Wives

1. Vicente Blasco Ibáñez, *Mexico in Revolution*, pp. 175–176; I. J. Bush, *Gringo Doctor*, p. 177; Timothy G. Turner, *Bullets, Bottles and Gardenias*, p. 49.

2. Thomas Janvier, *The Armies of Today*, p. 388.

3. Julio Guerrero, *La génesis del crimen en México*, p. 764; Henry C. Schmidt, *The Roots of Lo Mexicano: Self and Society in Mexican Thought, 1900–1934*, pp. 41, 51, 56.

4. Guerrero, *La génesis del crimen en México*, p. 764.

5. Ibid.

6. Alfredo Mirande and Evangelina Enríquez, *La Chicana: The Mexican-American Woman*, p. 82.

7. James W. Brown, *Heriberto Frías*, pp. 21, 42.

8. Heriberto Frías, *Tomochic*, p. 11.

9. Luis M. Garfías, *The Mexican Revolution: A Historic Politico-Military Compendium*, p. 7; Edwin Lieuwen, *Mexican Militarism: The Rise and Fall of the Revolutionary Army, 1910–1940*, p. 4.

10. Katz quoted in Eric R. Wolf, *Peasant Wars of the Twentieth Century*, pp. 31, 35; Carleton Beals, *Mexico: An Interpretation*, p. 196.

11. Rosa E. King, *Tempest Over Mexico: A Personal Chronicle*, pp. 93–94.

12. John Reed, *Insurgent Mexico*, p. 64.

13. Ibid., p. 189.

14. George S. Patton, *The Patton Papers, 1885–1940*, p. 303.

15. Herman Whitaker, "Villa and His People," *Sunset, the Pacific Monthly* 33, no. 2 (1914): 257.

16. It is practically impossible to estimate accurately the number of *soldaderas* serving in most large or small factions or rebel bands. Women, like men, changed sides constantly. Some groups had no *soldaderas* while some groups of female soldiers did not allow men in their brigades.

17. Edith O'Shaughnessy, *A Diplomat's Wife in Mexico*, p. 58.

18. Miguel Garibay, "The Revolution," in *Memories for Tomorrow*, ed. Margaret Beeson, Marjorie Adams, and Rosalie King, p. 1.

19. Will B. Davis, *Experiences and Observations of an American Consular Officer during the Mexican Revolution*, pp. 171–172.

20. Oscar J. Martínez, *Fragments of the Mexican Revolution: Personal Accounts from the Border*, p. 243.

21. Elsie González, "My Grandmother's Courage," in *Memories for Tomorrow*, ed. Beeson, Adams, and King, p. 2.

22. Martínez, *Fragments of the Mexican Revolution*, p. 259.

23. Ibid., p. 232.

24. María Linda Apodaca, "The Chicana Woman: An Historical Materialist Perspective," *Latin American Perspectives* 4, nos. 1 & 2 (Winter–Spring 1977): 83.

25. Martínez, *Fragments of the Mexican Revolution*, p. 228.

26. Maud Kenyon-Kingdon, *From Out of the Dark Shadows*, p. 51.

27. María Barron del Avellano, "Habla Elisa, heroína parralense,"

Sociedad Chihuahuense de Estudios Historicos, September 29, 1971, p. 16. She was born June 14, 1903, to Don Juan Alberto Grienssen and Doña Lucía Zamorano (Angel Rivas López, *El verdadero Pancho Villa,* p. 262).

28. John Womack, Jr., *Zapata and the Mexican Revolution,* p. 16.

29. Henry Baerlein, *Mexico, the Land of Unrest,* pp. 261, 271; King, *Tempest over Mexico,* p. 274.

30. Meyer and Sherman, *The Course of Mexican History,* p. 555.

31. I. Thord-Gray, *Gringo Rebel,* p. 211.

32. Nicolás Durán, in *Those Years of the Revolution, 1910–1920: Authentic Bilingual Life Experiences as Told by Veterans of the War,* ed. Esther R. Perez, James Kallas, and Nina Kallas, p. 156.

33. Ibid.

34. Archivo de la Palabra del Instituto Nacional de Antropología e Historia (hereafter INAH), Departamento de Estudios Contemporáneos, Programa de Historia Oral (hereafter PHO)/1/66, Francisco Ruiz Moreno, p. 22.

35. INAH, PHO/1/49, Major Justino López Estrada, p. 5.

36. INAH, PHO/1/41, Major Adán Uro García, p. 20; PHO/1/110, Major Constantino Caldero Vázquez, p. 28.

37. INAH, PHO/1/55, 1st Captain Jesús Herrera Calderón, p. 13; PHO/1/66, Dr. Francisco Ruiz Moreno, p. 22; PHO/1/155, General Manuel Mendoza, p. 29.

38. INAH, PHO/1/54, Captain Francisco Macías, p. 42; Durán, in *Those Years,* ed. Pérez, Kallas, and Kallas, p. 156; INAH, PHO/1/60, 1st Captain Jorge Ceceña Quiroz, pp. 21, 44, 46; Durán, in *Those Years,* ed. Pérez, Kallas, and Kallas, p. 157.

39. Verna Carleton Millan, *Mexico Reborn,* p. 153.

40. General Juan F. Azcárate, *Esencia de la Revolución,* p. 80; INAH, PHO/1/43, Sergeant Adalberto López Jara, p. 11.

41. INAH, PHO/1/116, Juan B. Rosales, p. 18; PHO/1/114, Colonel José Felipe Hernández Ortiz, p. 14; PHO/1/51, Ramón Caballero, p. 25; PHO/1/171, Cosme Pérez Flores, p. 19.

42. Reed, *Insurgent Mexico,* p. 134.

43. Luis Garfías M., *Truth and Legend of Pancho Villa,* p. 60.

44. Durán in *Those Years,* ed. Pérez, Kallas, and Kallas, p. 157.

45. Turner, *Bullets, Bottles and Gardenias,* p. 166.

46. Whitaker, "Villa," p. 252.

47. Edward Larocque Tinker, *The Memoirs of Edward Larocque Tinker,* p. 135.

48. Garfías, *Truth and Legend of Pancho Villa,* p. 143; quotation from INAH, PHO/1/98, Major Silvestre Cadena Jaramillo, p. 10; Dr. Cleofas Calleros, in *Pancho Villa,* ed. Jessie Peterson and Thelma Cox Knoles, pp. 33–34.

49. Peterson and Cox (eds.), *Pancho Villa,* pp. 33–34.

50. Ibid.

51. Lieutenant Angel Jiménez, interview, in *Those Years,* ed. Pérez, Kallas, and Kallas, p. 169.

52. Douglas W. Richmond, *Venustiano Carranza's Nationalist Struggle, 1893–1920*, p. 157.

53. INAH, PHO/1/130, Eulalio Mendoza, p. 53; Paco Ignacio Taibo I, *María Félix: 47 pasos por el cine*, p. 262.

54. INAH, PHO/1/180, Cosme Mendoza Chavira, p. 23.

55. Ibid; PHO/1/130, Eulalio Mendoza, p. 52; PHO/1/69, Major Médico Cirujano José Raya Rivera, p. 14.

56. Lucia Fox Lockert, *Chicanas: Their Voices, Their Lives*, p. 1. Lockert interviewed a woman named "Esperanza" who also named María Cadena as a female commander with followers. See also INAH, PHO/1/69, Raya Rivera, pp. 14–15.

57. INAH, PHO/1/69, Raya Rivera, pp. 14–15.

58. Manuel Calero, *Essay on the Reconstruction of Mexico*, p. 53.

59. Lieuwen, *Mexican Militarism*, p. 94.

60. David C. Bailey, *Viva Cristo Rey!: The Cristero Rebellion and the Church-State Conflict in Mexico*, p. 172. See also Jim Tuck, *The Holy War in Los Altos: A Regional Analysis of Mexico's Cristero Rebellion*, pp. 33, 114, 162.

61. Tuck, *The Holy War*, pp. 33, 114, 162.

62. Ibid., pp. 235–236.

63. Captain William S. Barrett, "Mexico and Revolution," *Infantry Journal* 36 (April 1930): 365, 369.

64. "Valentina Ramírez Avitia," *Magazine de Policía*, suppl., pp. 123–125.

65. Mario Gill, "Zapata: su pueblo y sus hijos," *Historia Mexicana* 2, no. 2 (October–December 1952): 309–310.

66. Consuelo Colón (ed.), *Las mujeres de México*, pp. 301–307.

4. In the Thick of the Fray

1. Blasco Ibáñez, *Mexico in Revolution*, p. 173; Kenneth J. Grieb, *The United States and Huerta*, pp. 66–68; Clarence C. Clendenen, *The United States and Pancho Villa*, p. 57; Michael C. Meyer, *Mexican Rebel: Pascual Orozco and the Mexican Revolution, 1910–1915*, pp. 95, 104–109.

2. Captain George H. Estes, "The Internment of Mexican Troops in 1914," *Infantry Journal* 11 (July–August 1915): 54.

3. Reed, *Insurgent Mexico*, p. 30.

4. Meyer, *Mexican Rebel*, p. 105.

5. Reed, *Insurgent Mexico*, pp. 188–189.

6. Estes, "Internment," May–June, p. 749.

7. National Archives (hereafter NA), Washington, D.C., Adjutant General's Office (hereafter AGO), Record Group (RG) 94, "Daily Diary of Events," 20081188, pp. 5, 9; *New York Times* (January 12, 1914).

8. *Los Angeles Times*, January 12, 1914; NA, AGO, RG 94, Telegram no. 43, 2024012.

9. Ernest Bicknell, *Pioneering with the Red Cross*, p. 158.

10. NA, Records of the Immigration and Naturalization Service (here-

after INS), RG 85, George Harris, Immigration Inspector to El Paso Station Inspector, February 24, 1914, 5012/336.

11. Louis C. Duncan, "The Wounded at Ojinaga," p. 436.

12. NA, AGO, RG 94, General Correspondence, June 22, 1914, 2118720.

13. NA, AGO, RG 94, January 12, 1914, Bliss to Agwar, 2008188.

14. Ibid., Wood to Bliss, 2008188/A286.

15. Estes, "Internment," July–August, p. 38.

16. Estes, "Internment," September–October, p. 16.

17. NA, AGO, RG 94, Fort Wingate Register Correspondence with Index by Name and Subject, 1-20-14 to 11-19-14, Entry 114, March 25, 1914, Colonel Enrique Pulido requests that his wife be allowed to return and live in Detention Camp; Entry 119, March 31, 1914, Captain José Quiroz requests authority for his two sisters to live in camp; Entry 131, permission for his family to enter camp on account of destitution.

18. Mendieta Alatorre, *La mujer en la Revolución mexicana*, pp. 77–78. In 1915 Carmen Parra landed in jail, an enemy of the Mexican government in power. Released in 1916, she returned to Chihuahua to join General Murgía. In 1919 she was given amnesty for her rebel activities as a follower of Pancho Villa. She died December 18, 1941, at the age of fifty-six. She was officially recognized as a veteran of the Revolution on January 5, 1942. For information about José Inés Salazar, see Ralph H. Vigil, "Revolution and Confusion: The Peculiar Case of José Inés Salazar," p. 152.

19. *El Paso Morning Times*, February 1, 1913.

20. NA, AGO, RG 94, file cards of prisoners at detention camp, 1914. Cimona Gallegos is listed on the file card for her husband/consort, Captain Federico Alonzo. Both were released from Fort Wingate in September 1914, and given train tickets to El Paso.

21. Peter B. Kyne, "With the Border Patrol," *Collier's Magazine*, May 9, 1914, p. 21.

22. Estes, "Internment," July–August, p. 44.

23. Ibid., p. 45; Kyne, "With the Border Patrol," p. 21; *El Paso Morning Times*, February 6, 1914.

24. Alan Knight, *The Mexican Revolution: Counter-revolution and Reconstruction*, vol. 2, p. 126.

25. Estes, "Internment," July–August, p. 45.

26. NA, AGO, RG 94, Return of Interned Mexican Prisoners, June 2, 1914, 2117935.

27. *El Paso Morning Times*, April, 19, 28, May 4, 1914; Estes, "Internment," September–October, p. 259; Salvador R. Mercado, *Revelaciones históricas*, p. 80.

28. Estes, "Internment," July–August, pp. 54–55.

29. NA, AGO, RG 94, Fort Wingate Register, Entry 151, May 23, 1914, n.p.

30. Estes, "Internment," July–August, p. 52; NA, AGO, RG 94, 2008188; Alberto J. Pani, *Hygiene in Mexico*, p. 10.

31. NA, AGO, RG 94, 2008188. The three *soldaderas* were Rosa González, Juana Torres, and María Hernández.

32. Estes, "Internment," July–August, p. 52.

33. Ibid., p. 40.

34. Ibid., September–October, p. 263.

35. Matthew T. Slattery, *Felipe Angeles and the Mexican Revolution*, pp. 131, 134.

5. We, the Women

1. Reed, *Insurgent Mexico*, p. 110.

2. Pozas, *Juan the Chamula: An Ethnological Re-Creation of the Life of a Mexican Indian*, pp. 39–40.

3. Pérez, Kallas, and Kallas (eds.), *Those Years*, p. 159.

4. Poniatowska, *Hasta no verte*, p. 20.

5. Macías, *Against All Odds*, pp. 42–43.

6. Lewis, *A Death*, pp. xi–xii.

7. Vivian M. Vallens, *Working Women in Mexico during the Porfiriato, 1880–1910*, p. 4.

8. Romo, "Y las soldaderas?" p. 12.

9. Quinn, *Original Sin*, p. 28.

10. Pérez, Kallas, and Kallas (eds.), *Those Years*, p. 161.

11. Kelley, *Yaqui Women*, pp. 157–159.

12. Ibid., pp. 130–132.

13. María Antonieta Rascón, "La mujer y la lucha social," p. 155.

14. Pérez, Kallas, and Kallas (eds.), *Those Years*, pp. 161, 170.

15. Poniatowska, *Hasta no verte*, p. 20; Macías, *Against All Odds*, p. 43.

16. Romo, "Y las soldaderas?" p. 12.

17. Lewis, *A Death*, p. xiv.

18. Pérez, Kallas, and Kallas (eds.), *Those Years*, p. 208.

19. Quinn, *Original Sin*, pp. 24, 28.

20. Kelley, *Yaqui Women*, p. 167.

21. Ibid., p. 142.

22. Macías, *Against All Odds*, pp. 40–43.

23. Pérez, Kallas, and Kallas (eds.), *Those Years*, pp. 163–164.

24. Ibid., p. 162.

25. Ibid., pp. 166, 171.

26. Poniatowska, *Hasta no verte*, p. 164.

27. Macías, *Against All Odds*, p. 43; Romo, "Y las soldaderas?" p. 13.

28. Lewis, *A Death*, p. 7.

29. Ibid., p. xvii.

30. Quinn, *Original Sin*, pp. 30–33.

31. Pérez, Kallas, and Kallas (eds.), *Those Years*, p. 208.

32. Ibid., pp. 163, 167.

33. Ibid., p. 170.

34. Poniatowska, *Hasta no verte*, p. 164.

35. Ibid., pp. 67–69, 107–108.

36. Macías, *Against All Odds*, p. 43.

37. Lewis, *A Death*, p. xxii.

38. Quinn, *Original Sin*, p. 32.

39. Paul J. Vanderwood, "Response to Revolt: The Counter-Guerrilla strategy of Porfirio Díaz," *Hispanic American Historical Review* 56 (November 1976): 573.

40. Kelley, *Yaqui Women*, p. 172.

41. Ibid., p. 144.

42. Macías, *Against All Odds*, p. 43.

43. Kelley, *Yaqui Women*, p. 172.

44. Ibid.

45. Poniatowska, *Hasta no verte*, pp. 1, 169.

46. Romo, "Y las soldaderas?" p. 14.

47. Ibid.

48. Lewis, *A Death*, p. x.

49. Pérez, Kallas, and Kallas (eds.), *Those Years*, p. 208.

50. Quinn, *Original Sin*, p. 23.

51. Pérez, Kallas, and Kallas (eds.), *Those Years*, pp. 57, 59, 80.

52. Ibid., pp. 178, 180–181.

53. Ibid., pp. 180, 187.

6. Adelita Defeats Juana Gallo

1. Abby Wettan Kleinbaum, *The War against the Amazons*, pp. 1, 5, 9, 39, 75–79, 112.

2. Estelle Irizarry, "Echos of the Amazon Myth in Medieval Spanish Literature," in *Women in Hispanic Literature*, ed. Beth Miller, p. 54.

3. Ibid.

4. Irving A. Leonard, "Conquerors and Amazons in Mexico," *Hispanic American Historical Review* 24 (November 1944): 564–565.

5. MacLachlan and Rodríguez O., *The Forging of the Cosmic Race*, p. 240.

6. As quoted in Leal, *Aztlán y México*, p. 185.

7. Brown, *Heriberto Frías*, p. 21; John S. Brushwood, "Heriberto Frías on Social Behavior and Redemptive Woman," *Hispania* 45 (May 1962): 250.

8. Mariano Azuela, *The Underdogs*, pp. 85, 110; Luis Leal, *Mariano Azuela*, p. 102.

9. Azuela, *The Underdogs*, p. 110.

10. Mariano Azuela, *Two Novels of Mexico: The Flies and the Bosses*, pp. 12, 43.

11. Ibid., p. 78.

12. Rafael Felipe Muñoz, *Relatos de la Revolucion: Antología*, pp. 50, 58.

13. Nellie Campobello, *Cartucho: relatos de la lucha en el norte de México*, p. 15.

14. Francisco L. Urquizo, *Tropa vieja*, pp. 20, 32, 56.

15. Michael Maccoby, "On Mexican National Character," in *Chicanos: Social and Psychological Perspectives*, ed. Nathaniel N. Wagner and Marsha J. Haug, p. 128.

16. Kessel Schwartz, *A New History of Spanish American Fiction from Colonial Times to the Mexican Revolution and Beyond*, p. 316.

17. Luis Leal, "Female Archetypes in Mexican Literature," in *Women in Hispanic Literature*, ed. Beth Miller, p. 230.

18. Francisco Rojas González, *La negra Angustias*, pp. 160, 192–193; Richard L. Jackson, *The Black Image in Latin American Literature*, p. 73.

19. Rojas González, *La negra Angustias*, pp. 192–193.

20. José Alvarado, "La Adelita es ahora Doña Adela," *Siempre*, November 24, 1954, p. 24.

21. Luis Zavalza Escandón, *Soldadera*, pp. 2–4.

22. Carlos Isla, *La Valentina*, pp. 7–10; idem, *La Adelita*, pp. 186–187.

23. Carlos Fuentes, *The Old Gringo*, p. 63.

24. Ibid., p. 114.

25. Ibid., p. 179.

26. Gilberto Vélez, *Corridos mexicanos*, p. 8.

27. Anita Brenner, *Idols behind Altars*, p. 209.

28. Soto, "The Mexican Woman," p. 80.

29. Andrés Henestrosa, ed., *Espuma y flor de corridos*, pp. 44–45.

30. Robert Redfield, *Tepoztlan, a Mexican Village: A Study of Folk Life*, p. 188.

31. Vélez, *Corridos*, p. 16.

32. Ibid., p. 44.

33. Ignacio Flores Muro, *La verdadera Juana Gallo*, p. 138.

34. Taibo I, *María Félix*, p. 262.

35. María Herrera-Sobek, "Mothers, Lovers, and Soldiers: Images of Woman in the Mexican Corrido," *Keystone Folklore* 23 (1979): 54.

36. *El Grito del Norte* 2 (July 6, 1969): 10; quotation from Vélez, *Corridos*, p. 56.

37. Romero Aceves, *La mujer en la historia de México*, p. 278; Vélez, *Corridos*, 37.

38. Baltasar Dromundo, *Francisco Villa y La "Adelita,"* p. 45.

39. Ibid.

40. Romo, "Y las soldaderas?" *Fem* 2 (1979): 12.

41. Vélez, *Corridos*, pp. 274–275.

42. Ibid.

43. Ibid.

44. "Yo me muero donde quiera" sung by Lola Beltrán.

45. Claes af Geijerstam, *Popular Music in Mexico*, p. 87.

46. Ibid.

47. *Las coronelas* played by Mariachi de América de Jesús R. de Hijar; *Las capitanas* played by Lalo García y su Conjunto.

48. "Las Adelitas" performed by Hermanas Padilla.

49. "Jesusita en Chihuahua, Juana Gallo, La Adelita" performed by Ballet Folklórico de Bellas Artes; Romo, "Y las soldaderas?" p. 12.

50. "Dónde estás, Adelita" sung by Lucha Villa; "La Adelita en hora 0" sung by Oscar Chávez.

51. Geijerstam, *Popular Music*, p. 54; Justino Fernández, *A Guide to Mexican Art*, p. 141.

52. Frederick C. Turner, *The Dynamics of Mexican Nationalism*, pp. 291–292.

53. Edmundo O'Gorman, Justino Fernández, Luis Cardoza (eds.), *Cuarenta siglos de plástica mexicana/Arte moderno y contemporáneo*, pp. 114–115.

54. Chicano Communications Center, *450 Years of Chicano History in Pictures*, p. 51; "Fragmento del proyecto revolución," *Mexico de Hoy* 7 (January 1955).

55. Shifra M. Goldman, *Contemporary Mexican Painting in a Time of Change*, p. 22; O'Gorman, Fernandez, and Cardoza (eds.), *Cuarenta siglos*, pp. 117–118, 135; Emily Edwards, *Painted Walls of Mexico from Prehistoric Times until Today*, p. 185; Azuela, *The Underdogs*, p. 51.

56. Casasola, *Historia gráfica*, vol. 1, p. 262; Ida Rodríguez Prampolini, *Juan O'Gorman, arquitecto y pintor*, p. 80.

57. Turner, *The Dynamics of Mexican Nationalism*, pp. 296, 298.

58. S. M. Eisenstein, *¡Qué Viva México!* pp. 78–82.

59. Harry M. Geduld and Ronald Gottesman (eds.), *Sergei Eisenstein and Upton Sinclair: The Making and Unmaking of Que Viva Mexico!* p. 150.

60. Ibid., p. 304.

61. William Harrison Richardson, *Mexico through Russian Eyes, 1806–1940*, pp. 248–249.

62. Emilio García Riera, *Historia documental del cine mexicano*, pp. 163, 184; José Natividad Rosales, "70 años en el drama de México," *Siempre*, August 23, 1972, pp. 45–46.

63. Carl Mora, *Mexican Cinema: Reflections of a Society, 1896–1980*, p. 78.

64. Taibo I, *María Félix*, p. 262.

7. *Soldaderas* in Aztlán

1. Camille Guerin-Gonzales, "Cycles of Immigration and Repatriation: Mexican Farm Workers in California Industrial Agriculture, 1900–1940," p. 2.

2. Ernesto Galarza, *Barrio Boy*, p. 112.

3. Quinn, *Original Sin*, p. 55.

4. Enrique López, "Back to Bachimba."

5. Adalberto Joel Acosta, *Chicanos Can Make It*, p. 8.

6. Enriqueta Longeaux y Vásquez, "The Mexican-American Woman," in *Sisterhood Is Powerful*, ed. Robin Morgan, p. 380.

7. Josephina Niggli, *Soldadera*, pp. 68, 94.

8. Ibid., pp. 65, 77, 90, 97–99, 109, 114; Carmen Salazar Parr and Genevieve M. Ramírez, "The Female Hero in Chicano Literature," in *Beyond Stereotypes*, ed. Maria Herrera-Sobek, pp. 49–50.

9. Jorge A. Huerta, *Chicano Theater: Themes and Forms*, p. 197.

10. Roberto J. Garza, "On with the Movement," *La Luz* 2 (May 1973): 34–36; Margarita B. Melville, "Female and Male in Chicano Theater," in *Mexican American Theatre*, ed. Nicolás Kanellos, p. 77.

11. Ana Montes, "Adelita," *Que Tal*, no. 26 (1976): 6–11; in 1981 *Voz de la Mujer* was performed by the San Jose chapter of Women in Teatro. This collage of poetry, songs, and speeches featured a segment of songs about

soldaderas and photos on stage of armed women. See Sue-Ellen Case, *Feminism and Theatre*, pp. 106–107.

12. Carlos G. Vélez-I., "The Raid," in *El Espejo*, ed. Octavio Ignacio Romano-V, p. 127.

13. Joe L. Navarro, "Stopover at Canacas," in *Yearnings*, ed. Albert C. Chavez, p. 48.

14. Roberta Fernández, "Zulema," in *Cuentos: Stories by Latinas*, ed. Alma Gomez, p. 214.

15. José Antonio Villarreal, *Pocho*, pp. 18, 126.

16. José Antonio Villarreal, *The Fifth Horseman*; Juan Bruce-Novoa, "Into the Breach: José Antonio Villarreal and the Fifth Horseman," *La Luz* 3 (January–February 1975): 31.

17. Richard Vásquez, *Chicano*, pp. 27–28, 32.

18. Ana Nieto Gómez, "Somos Chicanas de Aztlán," *La Raza* 2 (November 1969): 54.

19. Sylvia Alicia Gonzales, "La Chicana."

20. María Herrera-Sobek, "Abuelas revolucionarias," *Revista Chicano-Riqueña* 10 (Inveierno-Primavera 1982): 128.

21. Lorna Dee Cervantes, "Beneath the Shadow of the Freeway," in *Contemporary Chicana Poetry*, ed. Marta Ester Sánchez, p. 120.

22. Gloria Pérez, "Mi hombre," in *Voices of Aztlan*, ed. Dorothy E. Harth and Lewis M. Baldwin, pp. 183–184.

23. Ana Nieto Gómez, "Youth I Mirror," *La Raza* 2 (December 1969): 5.

24. Adela Marisela Ibarra, "Mexican Women in Folklore Dancing," p. 2; Elizabeth Sutherland Martínez and Enriqueta Longéaux y Vásquez, *Viva La Raza: The Struggles of the Mexican-American People*, p. 201.

25. Alan W. Barnett, *Community Murals: The People's Art*, pp. 66–67, 283–284.

26. Amalia Mesa-Baines, "La Nueva Chicana—A Profile of Santa Barraza," *Arriba*, October 1983, front cover, 5; Eliza May, "Carmen Rodríguez: Artist for Social Change," *Arriba*, December 1982, pp. 6–7.

27. Arthur G. Pettit, *Images of the Mexican American in Fiction and Film*, p. 224.

28. Allen L. Woll, *The Latin Image in American Film*, pp. 2, 4, 36.

29. Pettit, *Images of the Mexican American*, pp. 223–224.

30. Esteban Nájera, "Corrido de MAYO," *Magazin* 1 (April 1972): 51.

31. Armando R. Rendón, *Chicano Manifesto*, pp. 184, 189.

32. David F. Gómez, *Somos Chicanos*, p. 191.

33. Carlos Vásquez, "Women in the Chicano Movement," in *Mexican Women in the United States*, ed. Magdelena Mora and Adelaida R. del Castillo, p. 27.

34. Evangelina Enríquez and Alfredo Mirande, "Liberation Chicana Style: Colonial Roots of Feministas Chicanas," *De Colores* 4 (1978): 18.

35. Gema Matsuda, "La Chicana Organizes: The Comisión Femenil Mexicana in Perspective," *Regeneracion* 2 (1975): 27.

36. Velma Villa Romo, "Rape in the Barrio," *Comadre*, Fall 1978, p. 19.

37. Adelaida R. Del Castillo, "Malintzin Tenepal: A Preliminary Look

into a New Perspective," in *Essays on La Mujer,* ed. Rosaura Sánchez and Rosa Martínez Cruz, p. 139.

38. Norma Cantú, "Women Then and Now: An Analysis of the Adelita Image versus the Chicana as Political Writer and Philosopher," in *Chicana Voices,* p. 10.

39. Martha P. Cotera, "When Women Speak," in *Chicano Voices,* ed. Carlota Cárdenas de Dwyer, p. 101.

40. Isabelle Navar, "Como Chicana mi madre," *Encuentro Femenil* 1 (November 1973): 9.

41. Longeaux y Vásquez, "The Mexican-American Woman," p. 380.

42. Jennie V. Chávez, "Women of the Mexican American Movement," *Mademoiselle* 84 (April 1972): 152.

43. Esther Picazo, "Our Home in a Basket," in *La Mujer en Pie de Lucha,* p. 233.

44. María Terán, "Chicanas Reject Feminist Tokenism," *La Raza* 2 (November 1969): 4.

45. Guillermo Avila, "Luis Valdez," *Avance* 1 (1985): 8.

46. Ibid.

47. Yolanda Julia Broyles, "Women in El Teatro Campesino: Apoco Estaba Molacha La Virgen de Guadalupe?" in *Chicana Voices,* p. 183.

48. Katharine A. Díaz, "Corridos: A Review," *Caminos,* December 1984, 12.

Bibliography

Archival Material

Archivo de la Palabra del Instituto Nacional de Antropología e Historia (INAH), Departamento de Estudios Contemporáneos, Programa de Historia Oral (PHO), Mexico City.
Library of Congress, Manuscript Division, Washington, D.C.
Tasker Bliss Papers.
Hugh Scott Papers.
Leonard Wood Papers.
National Archives and Records Service (NA), Washington, D.C.
Records of the Immigration and Naturalization Service (INS), RG 85.
Records of the Adjutant General's Office (AGO), 1780s–1917, RG 94.

Interviews

Caballero, Ramón. Interview by Laura Espejel López, April 25, 1973, San Luis, Puebla, INAH, PHO/1/51.
Caldero Vázquez, Major Constantino. Interview by María Isabel Souza, October 27, 1973, Ciudad Chihuahua, Chihuahua, INAH, PHO/1/110.
Ceceña Quiroz, Captain Jorge. Interview by María Isabel Souza, July 12, 1973, Mexico City, INAH, PHO/1/60.
Hernández, Lieutenant Colonel José. Interview by María Isabel Souza, October 31, 1973, Ciudad Chihuahua, Chihuahua, INAH, PHO/1/114.
Herrera Calderón, Captain Jesús. Interview by María Isabel Souza, May 17, 1973, Mexico City, INAH, PHO/1/55.
López Estrada, Major Justino. Interview by América Teresa Briseño, May 29, 1973, Mexico City, INAH, PHO/1/49.
López Jara, Sergeant Adalberto. Interview by Laura Espejel López, February 20, 1973, Mexico City, INAH, PHO/1/43.

Macías, Captain Francisco. Interview by María Isabel Souza, January 22, 29, 1974, Mexico City, INAH, PHO/1/54.

Mendoza, Eulalio. Interview by Ximena Sepúlveda, February 11, 13, 1975, Tepepan, Xochimilco, INAH, PHO/1/130.

Mendoza, General Manuel. Interview by María Isabel Souza, June 30, 1974, Ciudad Chihuahua, Chihuahua, INAH, PHO/1/155.

Mendoza Chavira, Cosme. Interview by María Isabel Souza, July 3, 1974, Lerdo, Durango, INAH, PHO/1/160.

Pérez Flores, Cosme. Interview by Beatriz Arroyo Zacatelco, January 10, 1976, Tlaxcala, INAH, PHO/1/171.

Raya Rivera, Major Médico Cirujano José. Interview by María Isabel Souza, July 20, 1973, Parral, Chihuahua, INAH, PHO/1/69.

Rosales, Juan B. Interview by María Alba Pastor, October 25, 26, 1973, Ciudad Juárez, Chihuahua, INAH, PHO/1/116.

Ruiz Moreno, Dr. Francisco. Interview by María Isabel Souza, July 17, 1973, Ciudad Juárez, Chihuahua, INAH, PHO/1/66.

Uro García, Major Adán. Interview by Laura Espejel López, February 2, 1973, Mexico City, INAH, PHO/1/41.

Secondary Source Material

Acosta, Adalberto Joel. *Chicanos Can Make It*. New York: Vantage Press, 1971.

Alvarado, José. "La Adelita es ahora Doña Adela." *Siempre*, November 24, 1954, pp. 24–25.

Antón, Ferdinand. *La mujer en la América antigua*. Mexico City: Editorial Extemporáneos, 1975.

Apodaca, María Linda. "The Chicana Woman: An Historical Materialist Perspective." *Latin American Perspectives* 4, nos. 1, 2 (Winter–Spring 1977): 70–89.

Armijo, Lamberto. "Our Early Women—A Profile." *La Luz*, October–November 1979, p. 7.

Arrom, Silvia Marina. *The Women of Mexico City, 1790–1857*. Stanford, Calif.: Stanford University Press, 1985.

Avila, Guillermo. "Luis Valdez." *Avance* 1 (1983): 6–9.

Azcárate, General Juan F. *Esencia de la Revolución*. Mexico City: B. Costa-Amic, 1966.

Azuela, Mariano. *Two Novels of Mexico: The Flies and the Bosses*. Berkeley & Los Angeles: University of California Press, 1970.

———. *The Underdogs*. Translated by Edward Munguía, Jr. New York: New American Library of World Literature, 1915.

Baerlein, Henry. *Mexico, the Land of Unrest*. London: Herbert & Daniel, 1913.

Bailey, David C. *¡Viva Cristo Rey! The Cristero Rebellion and the Church-State Conflict in Mexico*. Austin: University of Texas Press, 1974.

Bancroft, Hubert H. *History of Mexico*. Vols. 2 (1571–1600), 3 (1600–1803). San Francisco, Calif.: A. L. Bancroft & Co., 1883–1886.

Barnett, Alan W. *Community Murals: The People's Art.* Philadelphia: Art Alliance Press, 1984.

Barrett, Captain William S. "Mexico and Revolution." *Infantry Journal* 36 (April 1930): 361–370.

Barron del Avellano, María. "Habla Elisa, heroína parralense." *Sociedad Chihuahuense de Estudios Históricos, Boletín,* September 29, 1971, pp. 15–17.

Beals, Carleton. *Mexico, an Interpretation.* New York: B. W. Huebsch, 1923.

Beeson, Margaret, Marjorie Adams, and Rosalie King, eds. *Memories for Tomorrow: Mexican-American Recollections of Yesteryear.* Detroit, Mich.: Blaine Ethridge, 1983.

Bernal, Ignacio. *Mexico before Cortés: Art, History, Legend.* Translated by Willis Barnstone. New York: Anchor Books, 1975.

Bicknell, Ernest P. *Pioneering with the Red Cross.* New York: Macmillan, 1935.

Blasco Ibáñez, Vicente. *Mexico in Revolution.* Translated by Arthur Livingston and José Padín. New York: E. P. Dutton, 1920.

Bolton, Herbert E. *Coronado: Knight of Pueblos and Plains.* New York: Whittlesey House, 1949.

Braddy, Haldeen. *Cock of the Walk: Legend of Pancho Villa.* Port Washington, N.Y.: Kennikat Press, 1970.

Brenner, Anita. *Idols behind Altars.* Boston: Beacon Press, 1929.

———. *The Wind That Swept Mexico: The History of the Mexican Revolution, 1910–1942.* Austin: University of Texas Press, 1971.

Brown, James W. *Heriberto Frías.* Boston, Mass.: Twayne, 1978.

Broyles, Yolanda Julia. "Women in El Teatro Campesino: Apoco Estaba Molacha la Virgen de Guadalupe?" In *Chicana Voices: Intersections of Class, Race and Gender,* pp. 162–187. Austin, Tex.: Center for Mexican American Studies Publications, 1986.

Bruce-Novoa, Juan. "Into the Breach: José Antonio Villarreal and the Fifth Horseman." *La Luz* 3 (January–February 1975): 31.

Brundage, Burr Cartwright. *The Fifth Sun: Aztec Gods, Aztec World.* Austin: University of Texas Press, 1979.

———. *A Rain of Darts: The Mexica Aztecs.* Austin: University of Texas Press, 1972.

———. *Two Earths, Two Heavens: An Essay Contrasting the Aztecs and the Incas.* Albuquerque: University of New Mexico Press, 1975.

Brushwood, John S. "Heriberto Frías on Social Behavior and Redemptive Women." *Hispania* 45 (May 1962): 249–253.

———. *Mexico in Its Novel: A Nation's Search for Identity.* Austin: University of Texas Press, 1966.

Burland, C. A. *The Gods of Mexico.* New York: G. P. Putnam's Sons, 1967.

———. *Montezuma, Lord of the Aztecs.* New York: G. P. Putnam's Sons, 1973.

Bush, I. J. *Gringo Doctor.* Caldwell, Idaho: Caxton Printers, 1939.

Calderón de la Barca, Frances Erskine. *Life in Mexico.* Berkeley & Los Angeles: University of California Press, 1982.

Calero, Manuel. *Essay on the Reconstruction of Mexico.* New York: De Laisne & Carranza, 1920.

Cameron, Charlotte. *Mexico in Revolution.* Philadelphia: J. B. Lippincott, 1925.

Campobello, Nellie. *Cartucho, relatos de la lucha en el norte de México.* Mexico City: Ediciones Integrales, 1940.

Candelaria, Cordelia. "La Malinche, Feminist Prototype." *Frontiers: A Journal of Women's Studies* 5 (Summer 1980): 1–6.

Caño, Gabriela. "El coronel Robles: Una combatiente zapatista." *Fem* 12, no. 64 (April 1988): 22–24.

Cantú, Norma. "Women Then and Now: An Analysis of the Adelita Image versus the Chicana as Political Writer and Philosopher." In *Chicana Voices: Intersections of Class, Race and Gender,* pp. 8–10. Austin, Tex.: Center for Mexican American Studies Publications, 1986.

Caruso, John Anthony. *The Liberators of Mexico.* Gloucester, Mass.: Peter Smith, 1967.

Casasola, Gustavo. *Historia gráfica de la Revolución, 1900–1970.* 10 vols. Mexico City: Editorial F. Trillas, 1960–1970.

Case, Sue-Ellen. *Feminism and Theatre.* New York: Methuen, 1988.

Caso, Alfonso. *The Aztecs: People of the Sun.* Translated by Lowell Dunham. Norman: University of Oklahoma Press, 1958.

———. *The Religion of the Aztecs.* Mexico City: Central News Co., 1937.

Cervantes, Lorna Dee. "Beneath the Shadow of the Freeway." In *Contemporary Chicana Poetry: A Critical Approach to an Emerging Literature,* ed. Marta Ester Sánchez, p. 120. Berkeley & Los Angeles: University of California Press, 1985.

Chamberlain, Samuel E. *My Confession.* 1855–1861. Reprint. New York: Harper & Brothers, 1956.

Chávez, Fray Angélico. *My Penitente Land.* Albuquerque: University of New Mexico Press, 1974.

Chávez, Jennie V. "Women of the Mexican American Movement." *Mademoiselle,* April 1972, pp. 82, 150–152.

"La Chicana: Our Unknown Revolutionaries." *El Grito del Norte,* June 5, 1971, p. 5.

Chicano Communications Center. *450 Years of Chicano History in Pictures.* Albuquerque: Chicano Communications Center, 1976.

Clendenen, Clarence C. *Blood on the Border: The United States Army and the Mexican Irregulars.* New York: Macmillan, 1969.

———. *The United States and Pancho Villa: A Study in Unconventional Diplomacy.* Ithaca, N.Y.: Cornell University Press, 1961.

Colón R., Consuelo. *Las mujeres de México.* Mexico City: Imprenta Gallards, I. A. Franco, 1944.

Cotera, Martha P. *Diosa y Hembra: The History and Heritage of Chicanas in the United States.* Austin, Tex.: Information Systems Development, 1976.

———. "When Women Speak." In *Chicano Voices,* ed. Carlota Cárdenas de Dwyer, pp. 100–104. Boston: Houghton Mifflin.

Dabbs, Jack Autrey. *The French Army in Mexico, 1861–1867: A Study of Military Government.* The Hague: Mouton, 1963.

Davis, Will B. *Experiences and Observations of an American Consular Officer during the Mexican Revolution.* Chula Vista, Calif.: Wayside Press, 1920.

Decker, Robert, and Esther Márquez. *The Proud Mexicans.* New York: Regents Publishing Co., 1973.

De la Peña, José Enrique. *With Santa Anna in Texas.* Edited and translated by Carmen Perry. 1836. Reprint. College Station: Texas A&M University Press, 1975.

Del Castillo, Adelaida R. "Malintzin Tenepal: A Preliminary Look into a New Perspective." In *Essays on la Mujer,* ed. Rosaura Sánchez and Rosa Martínez Cruz, pp. 124–149. Los Angeles: University of California–Los Angeles, Chicano Studies Center Publication, 1977.

De Shields, James T. *Tall Men with Long Rifles.* San Antonio: Naylor, 1935.

Díaz, Katharine A. "Corridos: A Review." *Caminos,* December 1984, p. 12.

Díaz del Castillo, Bernal. *The Discovery and Conquest of Mexico, 1517–1521.* Translated by J. M. Cohen. 1586. Reprint. Middlesex, Eng.: Penguin Books, 1963.

Diccionario enciclopédico de la lengua española. Vol. 2. Madrid: Gaspar y Roig Editores, 1872.

Dromundo, Baltasar. *Francisco Villa y La "Adelita."* Durango: Victoria de Durango, 1936.

Dulles, Foster Rhea. *The American Red Cross: A History.* New York: Harper & Bros., 1950.

Duncan, Louis C. "The Wounded at Ojinaga." *Military Surgeon* 34 (May 1914): 411–440.

Dunn, H. H. *The Crimson Jester.* New York: National Travel Club, 1934.

Durán, Fray Diego. *The Aztecs: The History of the Indies of New Spain.* Translated by Doris Heyden and Fernando Horcasitas. 1581. Reprint. New York: Orion Press, 1964.

———. *Book of the Gods and Rites and the Ancient Calendar.* Translated and edited by Fernando Horcasitas and Doris Heyden. 1581. Reprint. Norman: University of Oklahoma Press, 1971.

Edwards, Emily. *Painted Walls of Mexico from Prehistoric Times until Today.* Austin: University of Texas Press, 1966.

Eisenstein, Sergei M. *¡Qué viva México!* Mexico City: Ediciones Era, 1971.

Enríquez, Evangelina, and Alfredo Mirande. "Liberation Chicana Style: Colonial Roots of Feministas Chicanas." *De Colores* 4 (1978): 7–21.

Erauso, Catalina de. *Historia de la monja alférez.* 1624. Reprint. Madrid: Typográfica Renovación, 1918.

Estes, Captain George H. "The Internment of Mexican Troops in 1914." *Infantry Journal* 11 (May–June; July–August; September–October 1915): 747–769; 38–57; 243–264.

Expedition into New Mexico Made by Antonio de Espejo, 1582–1583 as Revealed in the Journal of Diego Pérez de Luxán, a Member of the Party.

Translated by George P. Hammond and Agapito Rey. Los Angeles: Quivira Society, 1929.

"Feminismo." In *Enciclopedia de México*, vol. 6 (1970), pp. 83–98.

Fernández, Justino. *A Guide to Mexican Art: From Its Beginning to the Present*. Translated by Joshua C. Taylor. Chicago: University of Chicago Press, 1961.

Fernández, Roberta. "Zulema." In *Cuentos: Stories by Latinas*, ed. Alma Gómez, Cherrie Moraga, and Mariana Romo-Carmona, pp. 212–226. New York: Kitchen Table Women of Color Press, 1983.

Fernández de Lizardi, José Joaquín. *Heroínas mexicanas*. Mexico City: Vargas Rea, 1955.

Figueroa Torres, J. Jesús. *Doña Marina: Una india ejemplar*. Mexico City: B. Costa-Amic, 1975.

Fisher, Lillian Estelle. "The Influence of the Present Mexican Revolution upon the Status of Mexican Women." *Hispanic American Historical Review* 22 (February 1942): 211–228.

Flores Muro, Ignacio. *La verdadera Juan Gallo*. Mexico City: 1969.

Foote, Cheryl J., and Sandra K. Schackel. "Indian Women of New Mexico: 1535–1680." In *New Mexico Women: Intercultural Perspectives*, ed. Joan Jensen and Darlis A. Miller, pp. 17–40. Albuquerque: University of New Mexico Press, 1986.

Foppa, Tito. *La tragedia mexicana*. Barcelona: Buigas Pons y Craj., n.d.

Formoso de Obregón Santacilia, Adela. *La mujer mexicana en la organización social del país*. Mexico City: Talleres Gráficos de la Nación, 1939.

"Fragmento del proyecto revolución." *México de Hoy* 7 (January 1955).

Frías, Heriberto. *Tomochic*. Mexico City: Editorial Porrúa, 1896.

Fuentes, Carlos. *The Old Gringo*. Translated by Margaret Sayers Peden. New York: Farrar, Straus & Giroux, 1985.

Fuentes, Patricia de, ed. and trans. *The Conquistadors: First Person Accounts of the Conquest of Mexico*. New York: Orion Press, 1963.

Fulton, Maurice Garland, ed. *Diary and Letters of Josiah Gregg: Excursions in Mexico and California, 1847–1850*. Norman: University of Oklahoma Press, 1944.

Galarza, Ernesto. *Barrio Boy*. Notre Dame, Ind.: University of Notre Dame Press, 1971.

García, Mario. *Desert Immigrants: The Mexicans of El Paso, 1880–1920*. New Haven, Conn.: Yale University Press, 1980.

García Riera, Emilio. *El cine mexicano*. Mexico City: Ediciones Era, 1963.

García Riera, Emilio, and Fernando Macotela. *La guía del cine mexicano de la pantalla grande a la televisión, 1919–1984*. Mexico City: Editorial Patria, 1984.

———. *Historia documental del cine mexicano*. 10 vols. Mexico City: Ediciones Era, 1969.

Gardiner, Henry C. *Martín López: Conquistador Citizen of Mexico*. Lexington: University of Kentucky Press, 1958.

Garfías, Luis M. *The Mexican Revolution: A Historic Politico-military Compendium*. Translated by Ana María Jolly de Espinosa. Mexico City: Ediciones Lara, 1979.

———. *Truth and Legend of Pancho Villa.* Translated by David Castledine. Mexico City: Panorama Editorial, 1981.

Garibay, Miguel. "The Revolution." In *Memories for Tomorrow: Mexican-American Recollections of Yesteryear,* ed. Margaret Beeson, Marjorie Adams, and Rosalie King, p. 1. Detroit: Blaine Ethridge, 1983.

Garza, Roberto J. "On with the Movement." *La Luz* 2 (May 1973): 34–36.

Geduld, Harry M., and Ronald Gottesman, eds. *Sergei Eisenstein and Upton Sinclair: The Making and Unmaking of Que Viva Mexico!* Bloomington: Indiana University Press, 1970.

Geijerstam, Claes af. *Popular Music in Mexico.* Albuquerque: University of New Mexico Press, 1976.

Gill, Mario. "Teresa Urrea, la Santa de Cabora." *Historia Mexicana* 6 (April–June 1951): 626–644.

———. "Zapata: Su pueblo y sus hijos." *Historia Mexicana* 2, no. 2 (October–December 1952): 294–312.

Gillmor, Frances. *The King Danced in the Marketplace.* Salt Lake City: University of Utah Press, 1977.

Goldman, Shifra M. *Contemporary Mexican Painting in a Time of Change.* Austin: University of Texas Press, 1977.

Gonzales, Sylvia Alicia. "La Chicana." In *La Chicana Piensa: The Social-Cultural Consciousness of a Mexican American Woman,* p. 66. N. p., 1974.

González, Elsie. "My Grandmother's Courage." In *Memories for Tomorrow: Mexican-American Recollections of Yesteryear,* Margaret Beeson, Marjorie Adams, and Rosalie King, p. 5. Detroit: Blaine Ethridge, 1983.

González A. Alpuche, Juan. "La Revolución." *Artes de México* 14, nos. 88–89 (1967): 65.

González Obregón, Luis. *Episodios de la guerra de independencia.* Mexico City: Secretaría de Educación Pública, 1945.

———. *The Streets of Mexico.* Translated by Blanche Collet Wagner. San Francisco: George Fields, 1937.

———. *La vida de México en 1810.* Mexico City: Editorial Innovación, 1911.

González Peña, Carlos. *History of Mexican Literature.* Translated by Gusta Barfield Nance and Florence Johnson Dunstan. Dallas: Southern Methodist University Press, 1943.

Gómez, David F. *Somos Chicanos: Struggles in Our Own Land.* Boston: Beacon Press, 1973.

Grieb, Kenneth J. *The United States and Huerta.* Lincoln: University of Nebraska Press, 1969.

Guerin-Gonzales, Camille. "Cycles of Immigration and Repatriation: Mexican Farm Workers in California Industrial Agriculture, 1900–1940." Ph.D. dissertation, University of California, Riverside, 1985.

Guerrero, Julio. *La génesis del crimen en México.* Paris: Librería de la Vda. de Ch. Bouret, 1901.

Guzmán, Martín Luis. *The Eagle and the Serpent.* Translated by Harriet de Onís. Gloucester, Mass.: Peter Smith, 1928.

Hacker, Barton C. "Women and Military Institutions in Early Modern

Europe: A Reconnaissance." *Signs: Journal of Women in Culture and Society* 6 (1981): 643–671.

Hague, Eleanor. *Spanish-American Folk-Songs.* New York: American Folk-Lore Society, 1917.

Hall, Oakley M. *The Adelita.* New York: Doubleday, 1975.

Hamilton, Lester. *Goliad Survivor: Isaac D. Hamilton.* San Antonio: Naylor, 1971.

Haring, D. H. *The Spanish Empire in America.* New York: Harcourt & World, 1947.

Hassig, Ross. *Aztec Warfare: Imperial Expansion and Political Control.* Norman: University of Oklahoma Press, 1988.

Hefter, J., ed. *El soldado mexicano; organización, vestuario, equipo. The Mexican Soldier; organization, dress, equipment, 1837–1847.* Mexico City: Ediciones Nieto-Brown-Hefter, 1958.

Henestrosa, Andrés. "La soldadera." In *Espuma y flor de corridos mexicanos,* pp. 44–45. Mexico City: Editorial Porrúa, 1977.

Hernández, Carlos. *Mujeres célebres de México.* San Antonio: Casa Editorial Lozano, 1918.

Herrera, Celia. *Francisco Villa, ante la historia.* Mexico City: Costa-Amic, 1939.

Herrera-Sobek, María. "Abuelas revolucionarias." *Revista Chicano-Riqueña* 10 (Winter–Spring 1982): 128.

———. "Mothers, Lovers, and Soldiers: Images of Woman in the Mexican Corrido." *Keystone Folklore Journal* 23 (1979): 53–76.

Herrera y Tordesillas, Antonio de. *The General History of the Vast Continent and Islands of America.* Vols. 2, 3. Translated by Captain John Stevens. 1559–1625. Reprint. London, 1740.

Horcasitas, Fernando, and Douglas Butterworth. "La Llorona." *Tlalocan* 4 (1963): 204–224.

Huerta, Jorge A. *Chicano Theater: Themes and Forms.* Ypsilanti, Mich.: Bilingual Press, 1982.

Ibarra, Adela Marisela. "Mexican Women in Folklore Dancing." University of California–Santa Barbara, 1986.

Inclán, Luis Gonzaga. *Astucia, el jefe de las hermanas de la hoja o los charros contrabandistas de la rama.* Vol. 2. 1864. Reprint. Mexico City: Editorial Porrúa, 1946.

Irizarry, Estelle. "Echoes of the Amazon Myth in Medieval Spanish Literature." In *Women in Hispanic Literature: Icons and Fallen Idols,* ed. Beth Miller, pp. 53–66. Berkeley & Los Angeles: University of California Press, 1983.

Isla, Carlos. *La Adelita.* Mexico City: Ediciones ELA, 1981.

———. *La Valentina.* Mexico City: Colección Paladines Mexicanas, 1980.

Isoldi, Gerardo de. "Las 'Adelitas' de la Revolución." *Hoy,* November 25, 1944, pp. 22–26.

Ixtlilxochitl, Don Fernando de Alva. *Historia chichimeca.* Mexico City: 1892.

Jackson, Richard L. *The Black Image in Latin American Literature.* Albuquerque: University of New Mexico Press, 1976.

Jacobs, Ian. *Ranchero Revolt: The Mexican Revolution in Guerrero.* Austin: University of Texas Press, 1982.

Janvier, Thomas A. *The Armies of Today.* New York: Harper & Bros., 1893.

Jaquette, Jane S. "Women in Revolutionary Movements in Latin America." *Journal of Marriage and the Family* 35 (May 1973): 344–354.

Jensen, Joan M., and Darlis A. Miller. *New Mexico Women: Intercultural Perspectives.* Albuquerque: University of New Mexico Press, 1986.

Johannsen, Robert W. *To the Halls of the Montezumas: The Mexican War in the American Imagination.* New York: Oxford University Press, 1985.

Johnson, Harry Prescott. "Diego Martínez de Hurdaide: Defender of the Northwestern Frontier of New Spain." *Pacific Historical Review* 11, no. 2 (June 1942): 169–185.

Kelley, Jane Holden. *Yaqui Women: Contemporary Life Histories.* Lincoln: University of Nebraska Press, 1978.

Kenyon-Kingdon, Maud. *From Out of the Dark Shadows.* San Diego, Calif.: Press of Frye and Smith, 1925.

King, Rosa E. *Tempest over Mexico: A Personal Chronicle.* Boston: Little, Brown, 1938.

Kissam, Edward, and Michael Schmidt, trans. *Poems of the Aztec Peoples.* Ypsilanti, Mich.: Bilingual Press, 1983.

Kleinbaum, Abby Wettan. *The War against the Amazons.* New York: McGraw-Hill, 1983.

Knight, Alan. *The Mexican Revolution: Counter-Revolution and Reconstruction.* Vol. 2. Cambridge: At the University Press, 1986.

Kyne, Peter B. "With the Border Patrol." *Collier's Magazine,* May 9, 1914, pp. 20–22.

La Chrisx. "La loca de la raza cósmica." *Comadre,* Spring 1978, pp. 5–9.

Lafaye, Jacques. *Quetzalcoatl and Guadalupe: The Formation of Mexican National Consciousness, 1531–1813.* Translated by Benjamin Keen. Chicago: University of Chicago Press, 1974.

Lampe, Philip E. "Our Lady of Guadalupe and Ethnic Prejudice." *Borderlands Journal* 9, no. 1 (Spring 1986): 91–120.

Langellier, John Philips, and Katherine Meyers Peterson. "Lancers and Leather Jackets: Presidial Forces in Spanish Alta California, 1769–1821." *Journal of the West* 20 (October 1981): 3–11.

Leal, Luis. *Aztlán y México: Perfiles literarios e históricos.* Binghampton, N.Y.: Bilingual Press, Editorial Bilingüe, 1985.

———. "Female Archetypes in Mexican Literature." In *Women in Hispanic Literature: Icons and Fallen Idols,* ed. Beth Miller, pp. 227–242. Berkeley & Los Angeles: University of California Press, 1983.

———. *Mariano Azuela.* New York: Twayne, 1971.

Lemprière, Charles. *Notes in Mexico in 1861 and 1862.* London: Longman, Green, Longman, Roberts & Green, 1862.

Leonard, Irving A. "Conquerors and Amazons in Mexico." *Hispanic American Historical Review* 24 (November 1944): 561–579.

León-Portilla, Miguel. *Aztec Thought and Culture: A Study of the Ancient Nahuatl Mind.* Translated by Jack Emory Davis. Norman: University of Oklahoma Press, 1963.

————, ed. *The Broken Spears: The Aztec Account of the Conquest of Mexico.* Boston: Beacon Press, 1962.

Lewis, Oscar. *A Death in the Sanchez Family.* New York: Vintage Books, 1969.

Lieuwen, Edwin. *Mexican Militarism: The Rise and Fall of the Revolutionary Army, 1910–1940.* Albuquerque: University of New Mexico Press, 1968.

Lockert, Lucia Fox. *Chicanas: Their Voices, Their Lives.* Lansing: Michigan State Board of Education, 1988.

————. "Elena Poniatowska: Hasta No Verte Jesús Mío." In *Women Novelists in Spain and Spanish America*, pp. 260–277. Metuchen, N.J.: Scarecrow Press, 1979.

Longeaux y Vásquez, Enriqueta. "The Mexican-American Woman." In *Sisterhood Is Powerful: An Anthology of Writings from the Women's Liberation Movement*, ed. Robin Morgan. New York: Vintage Books, 1970.

López, Enrique. "Back to Bachimba." *Horizon* 9 (Winter 1967): 51–58.

Love, Edgar F. "Negro Resistance to Spanish Rule in Colonial Mexico." *Journal of Negro History* 52 (April 1967): 98.

Maccoby, Michael. "On Mexican National Character." In *Chicanos: Social and Psychological Perspectives*, ed. Nathaniel N. Wagner and Marsha J. Haug, pp. 123–131. St. Louis: C. V. Mosby, 1971.

Macías, Anna. *Against All Odds: The Feminist Movement in Mexico to 1940.* Westport, Conn.: Greenwood Press, 1982.

MacLachlan, Colin M., and Jaime E. Rodríguez O. *The Forging of the Cosmic Race.* Berkeley & Los Angeles: University of California Press, 1980.

"La Malinche." In *Enciclopedia de México*, vol. 8 (1972), p. 234.

Martínez, Oscar J. *Fragments of the Mexican Revolution: Personal Accounts from the Border.* Albuquerque: University of New Mexico Press, 1983.

Martínez Sutherland, Elizabeth, and Enriqueta Longeaux y Vásquez. *¡Viva la Raza! The Struggles of the Mexican-American People.* New York: Doubleday, 1974.

Matsuda, Gema. "La Chicana Organizes: The Comisión Femenil Mexicana in Perspective." *Regeneración* 2 (1975): 25–27.

May, Eliza. "Carmen Rodríguez: Artist for Social Change." *Arriba*, December 1982, pp. 6–7.

Meier, Matt S. "María Insurgente." *Historia Mexicana* 23 (1973): 466–482.

Melville, Margarita B. "Female and Male in Chicano Theatre." In *Mexican American Theatre: Then and Now*, ed. Nicolás Kanellos, pp. 71–79. Houston: Arte Publico Press, Revista Chicano-Riqueña, 1983.

Mendieta Alatorre, Angeles. *La mujer en la Revolución mexicana.* Mexico City: Talleres Gráficos de la Nación, 1961.

Mercado, Salvador R. *Revelaciones históricas.* Las Cruces, N.M.: 1916.

Mesa-Baines, Amalia. "La Nueva Chicana—A Profile of Santa Barranza." *Arriba*, October 1983, p. 5.

Mexican Soldaderas and Workers during the Revolution: An Exhibition Catalogue. Santa Barbara: University of California, Center for Chicano Studies, 1979.

Meyer, Michael C. *Huerta: A Political Portrait*. Lincoln: University of Nebraska Press, 1972.

———. *Mexican Rebel: Pascual Orozco and the Mexican Revolution, 1910–1915*. Lincoln: University of Nebraska Press, 1972.

Meyer, Michael C., and William L. Sherman. *The Course of Mexican History*. New York: Oxford University Press, 1979.

Millan, Verna Carleton. *Mexico Reborn*. Boston: Houghton Mifflin. 1939.

Mirande, Alfredo, and Evangelina Enríquez. *La Chicana: The Mexican-American Woman*. Chicago: University of Chicago Press, 1979.

Montes, Ana. "Adelita." *Que Tal*, no. 26 (1976): 6–11.

Mora, Carl J. *Mexican Cinema: Reflections of a Society, 1896–1980*. Berkeley & Los Angeles: University of California Press, 1982.

Moreno, Daniel. *Batallas de la Revolución y sus corridos*. Mexico City: Editorial Porrúa, 1978.

Moreno, Dorinda, ed. *La mujer en pie de lucha: ¡Y la hora es ya!* Mexico City: Espina del Norte, 1973.

Muñoz, Rafael Felipe. *Relatos de la Revolución: Antología*. Mexico City: Ediciones Botas, 1934.

Muser, Curt. *Facts and Artifacts of Ancient Middle America*. New York: E. P. Dutton, 1978.

Nájera, Esteban. "Corrido de MAYO." *Magazin* 1 (April 1972): 51.

Nash, June. "The Aztecs and the Ideology of Male Dominance." *Signs* 4 (Winter 1978): 349–362.

Navar, Isabelle. "Como Chicana mi madre." *Encuentro Femenil* 1 (November 1973): 8–12.

Navarro, Joe L. "Stopover at Canacas." In *Yearnings*, ed. Albert C. Chávez, pp. 41–53. West Haven, Conn.: Pendulum Press, 1972.

Nicholson, Irene. *Firefly in the Night: A Study of Ancient Mexican Poetry and Symbolism*. London: Faber & Faber, 1959.

Nieto-Gómez, Anna. "Somos Chicanas de Aztlán." *La Raza* 2 (November 1969): 4.

———. "Women in Mexican History: Cinco de Mayo." *Somos*, May 1979, pp. 17–20.

———. "Youth I Mirror." *La Raza* 2 (December 1969): 5.

Niggli, Josephine. "Soldadera." In *Mexican Folk Plays*, ed. Frederick H. Koch, pp. 53–114. Chapel Hill: University of North Carolina Press, 1938.

Noguera, Eduardo. *Guide Book to the National Museum of Archeology, History and Ethnology*. Mexico City: Central News Co., 1938.

Nuevo diccionario ilustrado Sopena de la lengua española. Barcelona: Editorial Ramón Sopena, 1981.

O'Gorman, Edmundo, Justino Fernández, and Luis Cardoza, eds. *Cuarenta siglos de plástica mexicana/Arte moderno y contemporáneo*. Mexico City: Editorial Herrero, 1971.

O'Shaughnessy, Edith. *A Diplomat's Wife in Mexico*. New York: Harper & Bros., 1916.

O'Sullivan-Beare, Nancy. *Las mujeres de los conquistadores*. Madrid: Compañía Bibliográfica Española, 1956.

Palmer, Colin A. *Slaves of the White God: Blacks in Mexico, 1570–1650.* Cambridge, Mass.: Harvard University Press, 1976.

Pani, Alberto J. *Hygiene in Mexico.* Translated by Ernest L. de Gogorza. New York: G. P. Putnam's Sons, 1917.

Patton, George S. *The Patton Papers, 1885–1940.* Edited by Martin Blumenson. Boston: Houghton Mifflin, 1972.

Paz, Octavio. *The Labyrinth of Solitude: Life and Thought in Mexico.* Translated by Lysander Kemp. New York: Grove Press, 1961.

Pérez, Esther R., James Kallas, and Nina Kallas. *Those Years of the Revolution, 1910–1920: Authentic Bilingual Life Experiences as Told by Veterans of the War.* San Jose, Calif.: Aztlán Today, 1974.

Pérez, Gloria. "Mi hombre." In *Voices of Aztlán: Chicano Literature of Today,* ed. Dorothy E. Harth and Lewis M. Baldwin, pp. 183–184. New York: Mentor Books, 1974.

Pérez de Villagra, Gaspar. *History of New Mexico, 1610.* Translated by Gilberto Espinosa. Los Angeles: Quivira Society, 1933.

Peterson, Frederick. *Ancient Mexico: An Introduction to the Pre-Hispanic Cultures.* New York: G. P. Putnam's Sons, 1959.

———. "Women Warriors and Laughing Faces." *Natural History* 63 (May 1954): 210.

Peterson, Jessie, and Thelma Cox Knoles, eds. *Pancho Villa.* New York: Hastings House, 1977.

Pettit, Arthur G. *Images of the Mexican American in Fiction and Film.* College Station: Texas A&M University Press, 1980.

Philips, Rachael. "Marina/Malinche: Masks and Shadows." In *Women in Hispanic Literature: Icons and Fallen Idols,* ed. Beth Miller, pp. 97–114. Berkeley & Los Angeles: University of California Press, 1983.

Picazo, Esther. "Our Home in a Basket." In *La mujer en pie de lucha,* ed. Dorinda Moreno, pp. 233–235. Mexico City: Espina del Norte Publications, 1973.

Pinchon, Edgcumb. *Viva Villa!* New York: Arno Press, 1933.

———. *Zapata the Unconquerable.* New York: Doubleday, Doran & Co., 1941.

Plenn, J. H. "Forgotten Heroines of Mexico: Tales of the Soldaderas, Amazons of War and Revolution." *Travel* 68 (April 1936): 24.

Plunket, Irene L. *Isabel of Castile and the Making of the Spanish Nation, 1451–1504.* New York: G. P. Putnam's Sons, 1915.

Poniatowska, Elena. *Hasta no verte Jesús mío.* Mexico City: Ediciones Era, 1969.

Powell, Philip Wayne. *Soldiers, Indians, and Silver: The Northward Advance of New Spain, 1550–1600.* Berkeley & Los Angeles: University of California Press, 1952.

Pozas, Ricardo. *Juan the Chamula: An Ethnological Re-creation of the Life of a Mexican Indian.* Translated by Lysander Kemp. Berkeley & Los Angeles: University of California Press, 1952.

Prescott, William H. *The Portable Prescott: Rise and Decline of the Spanish Empire.* Edited by Irwin R. Blacker. New York: Viking, 1963.

Putnam, Frank Bishop. "Teresa Urrea, 'the Saint of Dabora.'" *Southern California Quarterly* 45 (September 1963): 245–264.

Quinn, Anthony. *The Original Sin*. Boston: Little, Brown, 1972.

Rascón, María Antonieta. "La mujer mexicana como hecho político: La precursora, la militante." *Siempre*, supplement, "La Cultura en México," January 3, 1973, pp. ix–xii.

———. "La mujer y la lucha social." In *Imagen y realidad de la mujer*, ed. Elena Urrutia, pp. 139–174. Mexico City: SepSetentas, 1975.

Redfield, Robert. *Tepoztlan, a Mexican Village: A Study of Folk Life*. Chicago: University of Chicago Press, 1930.

Reed, John. *Insurgent Mexico*. New York: International publishers, 1914.

Rendón, Armando B. *Chicano Manifesto*. New York: Collier Books, 1971.

Richardson, William Harrison. *Mexico through Russian Eyes, 1806–1940*. Pittsburgh: University of Pittsburgh Press, 1988.

Richmond, Douglas W. *Venustiano Carranza's Nationalist Struggle, 1893–1920*. Lincoln: University of Nebraska Press, 1983.

Rivas López, Angel. *El verdadero Pancho Villa*. Mexico City: B. Costa-Amic, 1970.

Robelo, Dr. Cecilio A. *Diccionario de mitología náhuatl*. Mexico City: Ediciones Fuente Cultural, 1904.

Rodríguez Prampolini, Ida. *Juan O'Gorman, arquitecto y pintor*. Mexico City: Universidad Nacional Autónoma de México, 1982.

Rojas González, Francisco. *La negra Angustias*. Mexico City: Edición y Distribución Ibero-Americano de Publicaciones, 1944.

Romero Aceves, Ricardo. *La mujer en la historia de México*. Mexico City: Costa-Amic, 1982.

Romo, Marta. "Y las soldaderas? Tomasa García toma la palabra." *Fem 2*, no. 4 (1979): 12–14.

Rosales, José Natividad. "70 años en el drama de México." *Siempre*, August 23, 1972, pp. 45–46.

Ruiz, Ramón Eduardo. *The Mexican War: Was It Manifest Destiny?* New York: Holt, Rinehart & Winston, 1963.

Rutherford, John. *Mexican Society during the Revolution: A Literary Approach*. London: Oxford University Press, 1971.

Sahagún, Fray Bernardino de. *Florentine Codex, General History of the Things of New Spain*. Bks. 2, 10. Translated by J. O. Anderson and C. E. Dibble. 1570. Reprint. Santa Fe, N.M.: School of American Research, 1981.

Salas, Angel. "La batalla del 5 de mayo en el Peñón." *Mexican Folkways* 8, no. 2 (April–June 1933): 56–82.

Salazar Parr, Carmen, and Genevieve M. Ramírez. "The Female Hero in Chicano Literature." In *Beyond Stereotypes: The Critical Analysis of Chicana Literature*, ed. María Herrera-Sobek, pp. 47–60. Binghampton, N.Y.: Bilingual Press/Editorial Bilingüe, 1985.

Salcedo Guerrero, Mario. "Vicente Guerrero's Struggle for Mexican Independence, 1810–1821." Ph.D. dissertation, University of California–Santa Barbara, 1977.

Sánchez, Marta Ester. *Contemporary Chicana Poetry: A Critical Approach to an Emerging Literature.* Berkeley & Los Angeles: University of California Press, 1985.

Santamaría, Francisco Javier. *Diccionario de mejicanismos.* 2d ed. Mexico City: Editorial Porrúa, 1974.

Santos, Richard G. *Santa Anna's Campaign against Texas, 1835–1836.* Salisbury, N.C.: Documentary Publications, 1981.

Schmidt, Henry C. *The Roots of Lo Mexicano: Self and Society in Mexican Thought, 1900–1934.* College Station: Texas A&M University Press, 1978.

Schroeder, Albert H., and Dan S. Matson. *A Colony on the Move: Gaspar Castaño de Sosa's Journal, 1590–1591.* Salt Lake City: School of American Research, 1965.

Schwartz, Kessel. *A New History of Spanish American Fiction from Colonial Times to the Mexican Revolution and Beyond.* Coral Gables: University of Miami Press, 1972.

Sejourne, Laurette. *Burning Water: Thought and Religion in Ancient Mexico.* New York: Vanguard Press, 1956.

Simmons, Merle E. *The Mexican Corrido as a Source of Interpretive Study of Modern Mexico, 1870–1950.* Bloomington: Indiana University Press, 1957.

Sisto, Augusto. *Mitos y leyendas mexicanos.* Mexico City: El Libro Español, 1963.

Slattery, Matthew T. *Felipe Angeles and the Mexican Revolution.* Parma Heights, Ohio: Greenbriar Books, 1986.

Smith, Donald D. *The Viceroy of New Spain.* Berkeley & Los Angeles: University of California Press, 1913.

Smith, George Winston, and Charles Judah, eds., *Chronicles of the Gringos: The U.S. Army in the Mexican War, 1846–1848.* Albuquerque: University of New Mexico Press, 1968.

El soldado mexicano, 1837–1847, organización, vestuario, equipo y reglamentos militares. Mexico City: Ediciones Nieto, Brown, Hefter, 1958.

Soto, Shirlene Ann. "The Mexican Woman: A Study of Her Participation in the Revolution, 1910–1940." Ph.D. dissertation, University of New Mexico, 1977.

Soustelle, Jacques. *Daily Life of the Aztecs on the Eve of the Spanish Conquest.* Translated by Patrick O'Brien. Palo Alto, Calif.: Stanford University Press, 1955.

Sten, María. *Las extraordinarias historias de los códices mexicanos.* Mexico City: Editorial Joaquín Mortiz, 1972.

———. *The Mexican Codices and Their Extraordinary History.* Mexico City: Editorial Joaquín Mortiz, 1972.

Stevenson, Robert. *Music in Mexico: A Historical Survey.* New York: Thomas Y. Crowell, 1952.

Taibo I., Paco Ignacio. *María Félix: 47 pasos por el cine.* Mexico City: Joaquín Mortiz Planeta, 1985.

Tejeira, Otilia Arosemena de. "The Women in Latin America: Past, Present, Future." *Américas,* supplement, 26 (April 1974): S1–S6.

Terán, María. "Chicanas Reject Feminist Tokenism." *La Raza* 2 (November 1969): 4.

Tezozomoc, Fernando Alvarado. "The Finding and Founding of Tenochtitlán from the Crónica Mexicayotl (1609)." Translated and with notes by Thelma D. Sullivan. *Tlalocan* 6, no. 4 (1971): 312–336.

Thord-Gray, I. *Gringo Rebel.* Coral Gables, Fla.: University of Miami Press, 1960.

Tinker, Edward Larocque. *The Memoirs of Edward Larocque Tinker.* Austin: University of Texas, 1970.

Torquemada, Fray Juan de. *Monarquía indiana.* Vol. 2. Mexico City: 1723.

Torres, Elías L. *Vida y hechos de Francisco Villa.* Mexico City: Editorial Epoca, 1975.

Treviño, Gloria. "Quien soy." *La Luz* 6 (March 1977): 18.

Tuck, Jim. *The Holy War in Los Altos: A Regional Analysis of Mexico's Cristero Rebellion.* Tucson: University of Arizona Press, 1982.

———. *Pancho Villa and John Reed: Two Faces of Romantic Revolution.* Tucson: University of Arizona Press, 1984.

Turner, Frederick C. *The Dynamics of Mexican Nationalism.* Chapel Hill: University of North Carolina Press, 1968.

———. "Los efectos de la participación femenina en la Revolución de 1910." *Historia mexicana* 64 (April–June 1967): 603–620.

Turner, Timothy G. *Bullets, Bottles, and Gardenias.* Dallas: South-West Press, 1935.

Uroz, Antonio. *Hombres y mujeres de México.* Mexico City: Editorial Lic. Antonio Oruz, 1974.

Urquizo, Francisco L. *Tropa vieja.* Mexico City: Talleres Gráficas del Departamento de Publicidad y Propaganda de la Secretaría de Educación Pública, 1943.

Valdez, Luis M. "Bernabé." In *Contemporary Chicano Theatre,* ed. Roberto J. Garza, pp. 191–204. Notre Dame, Ind.: University of Notre Dame Press, 1976.

"Valentina Ramírez Avitia." *Magazine de Policia,* supplement (n.d.), pp. 123–125.

Vallens, Vivian M. *Working Women in Mexico during the Porfiriato, 1880–1910.* San Francisco: R&F Research Associates, 1978.

Vanderwood, Paul J. "Response to Revolt: The Counter-Guerrilla Strategy of Porfirio Díaz." *Hispanic American Historical Review* 56 (November 1976): 551–579.

Vásquez, Carlos. "Women in the Chicano Movement." In *Mexican Women in the United States: Struggles Past and Present,* ed. Magdalena Mora and Adelaida R. del Castillo, pp. 27–28. Los Angeles: University of California–Los Angeles, Chicano Studies Research Center Publications, 1980.

Vásquez, Richard. *Chicano.* New York: Doubleday, 1970.

Vélez, Gilberto. *Corridos mexicanos.* Mexico City: Editores Mexicanos Unidos, 1982.

Vélez-I., Carlos G. "The Raid." In *El Espejo—The Mirror: Selected Mexican-American Literature,* ed. Octavio Ignacio Romano-V., pp. 125–127. Berkeley, Calif.: Quinto Sol, 1969.

Vigil, Ralph H. "Revolution and Confusion: The Peculiar Case of José Inés Salazar." *New Mexico Historical Review* 52, no. 2 (1978): 145–170.

Villarreal, José Antonio. *The Fifth Horseman*. New York: Doubleday, 1974.

———. *Pocho*. New York: Doubleday, 1959.

Wagner, Henry R. *The Rise of Fernando Cortes*. Berkeley, Calif.: Cortes Society, 1944.

Wax, Murray L. *Indian Americans: Unity and Diversity*. Englewood Cliffs, N.J.: Prentice-Hall, 1971.

Whitaker, Herman. "Villa and His People." *Sunset, the Pacific Monthly* 33, no. 2 (1914): 251–257.

Wilson, Robert Anderson. *A New History of the Conquest of Mexico*. Philadelphia: James Challen & Son, 1959.

Wolf, Eric R. *Peasant Wars of the Twentieth Century*. New York: Harper & Row, 1969.

———. *Sons of the Shaking Earth*. Chicago: University of Chicago Press, 1959.

Woll, Allen L. *The Latin Image in American Film*. Los Angeles: University of California–Los Angeles Latin American Center Publications, 1977.

Womack, John, Jr. *Zapata and the Mexican Revolution*. New York: Alfred A. Knopf, 1969.

Zavalza Escandón, Luis. *Soldadera*. Mexico City, 1951.

Zendejas, Adelina. *La mujer en la intervención francesa*. Mexico City: Sociedad Mexicana de Geografía y Estadística, 1962.

Films

La Adelita (1937).

The Alamo (1960).

Los amores de Marieta (1963).

La chamuscada (1967).

Las coronelas (1958).

La cucaracha (1958).

Enamorada (1946).

La escondida (1955).

Flor silvestre (1943).

La generala (1970).

La guerrillera de Villa (1967).

Juana Gallo (1960).

Juan Soldado (1949).

Lauro Puñales (1966).

Memorias de un mexicano (1950).

La negra Angustias (1949).

100 Rifles (1969).

The Professionals (1969).

La soldadera (1966).

La Valentina (1938, 1965).

Vera Cruz (1954).

Viva Villa (1934).
Viva Zapata (1952).
The Wild Bunch (1969).

Discography

La Adelita. Lucha Moreno, Ecos de la Revolución, DIMSA Records, DML 1003.
La Adelita en Hora O. Oscar Cháves, Polydor Records, LPR 16310.
Las Adelitas. Hermanas Padilla, Canciones de Campo, Camden Records, CAM s-14.
Las capitanas. Polkas con Lalo García y su Conjunto, OLA Records, OLP-5137.
Las coronelas. Mariachi de América de Jesús R. de Hijar, Ariola Records, ML-5006-B.
El corrido del norte. Lucha Moreno, Ecos de la Revolución, DIMSA Records, DML 1003.
Donde estás, Adelita. Lucha Villa con el mariachi Vargas, Musart Records, Ed-1783.
Jesusita en Chihuahua, Juana Gallo, La Adelita. Ballet Folklórico de Bellas Artes, Musart Records, ED-618.
María la Bandida. Mis corridos . . . José Alfredo Jiménez, Arcano Records, DKL 1-3075-B.
Marieta. Lucha Moreno, Ecos de la Revolución, DIMSA Records, DML 1003.
Mujeres valientes, Miguel Francisco Barragán. Si se puede, Pan-American Records, PA-101.
La rielera, Dueto las Pájaras y Conjunto los Trovadores del Norte. Camden Records, CAMS-422.
La Valentina, Poncho Villagómez, Del Bravo Records, BLP121.
Yo me muero donde quiera, Lola Beltrán, Peerless Records, ADP-517-2.

Index